Coal Dust in Our Veins

Life in Colorado Coal Country

1940 - 1970

Sixteen Tons

Some people say a man is made outta mud
A poor man's made outta muscle and blood
Muscle and blood and skin and bones
A mind that's a weak and a back that's strong

You load sixteen tons, what do you get?
Another day older and deeper in debt
Saint Peter don't you call me 'cause I can't go
I owe my soul to the company store

By Merle Travis

Made popular by Tennessee Ernie Ford

Coal Dust in Our Veins
Life in Colorado Coal Country 1940-1970

Copyright © 2021
All Rights Reserved

**Edited and Illustrated By
Lawrence M. Rutherford**

**Aquinas and More Publishing
Ft. Collins, Colorado 80926**
ISBN9780999413159

Contributors

Barbara (Rutherford) Martin, Fort Collins, Colorado

Marlene (Rutherford) Sutherland, Denver, Colorado

Lawrence Rutherford, Colorado Springs, Colorado

Edward Rutherford, Las Vegas, Nevada

Ralph Henderson, Marlene (Rutherford) Henderson, Ken Martin, Barbara (Rutherford) Martin, Mom, Dad, Lawrence Rutherford, Frances (Gastellum) Rutherford, Edward Rutherford, Patricia (McCormick) Rutherford
1986

Dedicated to
Our Children and Grandchildren

"To be born into a family is to inherit a legacy.........To remain close to one's extended family is to steep oneself in a cultural tradition and a storehouse of proverbial wisdom. To know one's family history is to feel a sense of indebtedness for all that has been transmitted and received from the immediate and distant past. To acknowledge a sense of gratitude for a glorious or noble heritage evokes a sense of humility--one understands that one is but a part of a whole, a single member of an extended, intergenerational family that spans centuries. This sense of family tradition and culture provides rootedness, a stability that allows for the fullness of human development in an environment that clarifies the purpose and meaning of one's life."

From New Oxford Review, April 2018 "The Family: The Center of Civilization" by Mitchell Kalpakgian

Disclaimer

The memories found in this book are as we recall them from 50 to 70 years ago. Other people may remember these recollected events in the book somewhat differently or from another perspective. The intent is to project an overall picture of the environment of the time and not necessarily an exact history of the time. It is also intended to provide a contrast to our contemporary era for the consideration of the reader. Our apologies to anyone who might find the details inaccurate.

Table of Contents

Prologue 1
   Coal Mining is in Our Blood 1
   Charles Clay Rutherford 3
   Ralph Rutherford 3
   Daisy (Squire) Rutherford 5
   Joseph L. Knez 6
   Mary (Mahovald) Knez 8
   Marie Rutherford: .... **Error! Bookmark not defined.**
   Mount Harris 11

Part One 13
BRIGADOON 13
   Our Town 14
      Uptown 15
      The Mines 20
      The Mine Tipple 20
      The Train 23
      The Yampa River 25
   Our Homes in Mt. Harris 29
      The Cinder Block House 29
      The Druggists House 35
      The Superintendent's House 38
   School in Mt. Harris 45
      The Grade School 45
      High School 54

Religion 59

    Father Prinster 60

    Sisters Placide and Columbiere 62

Home and Family 65

    Clothing and Fashion 65

    Entertainment 70

    Food and Hospitality 80

    Health and Illness 85

    Household Chores 92

    Christmas time 94

Community Activities 97

    Winter in Mt. Harris 97

    Colorful Personalities 100

    Rutherford Music 104

    Hunting and Fishing - Mt. Harris 108

    The Knez Ranch 110

Milner and Steamboat Springs 115

    The Milner Gas Station 115

    Driving to Steamboat Springs 116

    Steamboat Springs Swimming Pool 117

Relatives 119

    Grandparents 119

    Aunts, Uncles and Cousins 122

    The Car Accident on Wise Hill and Marie Carter 128

    Aunt Grace and Uncle Joseph 129

    The BB Gun and Tommy Joe 136

Mine Closing 137

End of an Era 137

Part Two 139
THE BIG CITY 139

Craig 141
Moving to Craig 143

School in Craig 145
Elementary School - Ed 145
High School – Ed 155
School – Larry 159

Life in Town 165
Dragging Main 165
Sherwood Forest 165
Dorothy and Joe Rotter 166
The Church Next Door 167
St. Michael's Parish 167
Learning to Drive – The Hard Way 169
Flower Garden and Grotto 170
Building and making things 171
Boy Scouts 173
Driving to Wyoming 174
Tragic Event 175

Winter in Craig 177
The Buck Peak Incident 177
A Toboggan Story 179
Buck Peak – Fun Times 180
Toboggan Crash on Buck Peak 181
Lost in a Blizzard 182

Snow in Steamboat Springs and on Rabbit Ears Pass 184

Hunting and Fishing in Craig 187

Working in Town 193

    Mowing lawns 193

    Working for Empire Energy 197

Life after High School 200

    College – Larry 200

    Military – Larry 212

Epilogue 217

Eulogy for Our Dad 217

Eulogy for Our Mom 219

Changing Times 223

Appendices 227

Appendix 1 - Rutherford Family Tree 228

Appendix 2 - Mahowald Family Tree 229

Appendix 3 - Squire Family Tree 230

Appendix 4 Rutherford/Knez Cousins 231

Appendix 5 – Children, Grand Children and Great Grand Children 232

Appendix 6 – Photo Album 233

Appendix 7 – Dad's Letter to Mom 240

Appendix 8 – Mom and Grandma Knez 241

Appendix 9 - Top Movies 1940 - 1970 244

Appendix 10 - Family Recipes 245

Appendix 11 Floor Plans 248

Appendix 12 - Photograph Credits 251

Prologue

Coal Mining is in Our Blood

"Come to me, all you who labor and are burdened, and I will give you rest." **Matthew 11:28**

Both Grandpa Joe Knez and Grandpa Charles "Coke" Rutherford were miners when we were growing up in Northwestern Colorado. Grandpa Knez farmed outside of Craig in the summer and mined coal from a mine on his property in the winter. Grandpa Rutherford worked in the Mt. Harris mine as did most of our Rutherford uncles.

Craig is only 24 miles west of Mt. Harris and we went there regularly to visit the Knez relatives. Steamboat Springs is 18 miles to the east of Mt. Harris and that is where our parish was.

Mount Harris was short lived compared to most towns. It opened in 1914 and closed in 1958--less than 50 years. It is surprising, then, that for so many who made their home there during that time the town has left such a fond impression in their minds and hearts.

Although its demise was gradual in the later years, once the decision to close and liquidate was made, it quickly disappeared like the village in the story, "Brigadoon." There are few visible signs of its existence left except to those people who had lived there in its past. For those driving by it is now just another peaceful valley along the Yampa River. The entire town has vanished among the trees and other foliage through the many years past.

Although this book recounts the story of the Rutherford family in Colorado Coal Country, its intent is to provide a general picture of what it was like to live in this area and in this era. It is a way of life that has disappeared much like the coal town of Mount Harris but deserves to be recollected and maybe resurrected in the current age.

Charles Clay Rutherford

Charles Clay Rutherford, better known as Coke Rutherford, was born in Indian Territory, near Tulsa, Oklahoma on April 14, 1895. Charles' father was William Robinson Rutherford born in Fayetteville, Arkansas, in 1854, and he died on October 10, 1918. His mother was Parthena Collyer Rutherford and she was born in Indiana in 1857 and died on March 6, 1923. His parents were married in Washington County, Arkansas, on October 18, 1879. William was a farmer but also followed work in the oil fields of Oklahoma. They had ten children. At one time, the Rutherfords had a huge plantation in Tennessee, but they sold it before the Civil War.

Grandpa and Grandma Rutherford at the Superintendent's House 1956

Charles came to Routt County, Colorado, with his brothers Tom and Albert. They moved there to help build the railroad from Mt. Harris to Hayden. The brothers later returned to Oklahoma but Charles stayed and made Routt County his home.

Genealogical History of the Rutherford Family compiled by William Kenneth Rutherford.

Ralph Rutherford: My Dad, Coke Rutherford, as everyone called him, worked at different jobs, mainly farming and mining and moved to Mt. Harris in 1914. They left the town for a few years, but returned again in 1923 and made it their home until 1953. Coke worked at Curtis Gulch, south of Milner. Both mines there went broke, in fact, he didn't even get his last paycheck. They then moved to Milner around 1924. Afterward they moved back to Mt. Harris and Dad loaded coal there. They were paid by the ton then instead of the hour, only about 90 cents a ton. Sometimes he would load about 20 tons a day in a nine hour day depending on how many pit cars were available. Coke worked in the mine for 10 years and fired boilers in the old power plant for three years. He also was a welder for the company (Colorado and Utah Coal) and was a lamp man at one time.

Coke and Daisy Rutherford on their Wedding Day

Daisy (Squire) Rutherford

Daisy (Squire) Rutherford was born on the Squire Ranch at Morgan bottom near Mt. Harris, Colorado, on May 11, 1896. Her father was Albert Squire who was born in Devonshire, England, on April 7, 1853, and he set sail for this country on June 5, 1872. He resided for a short time in New Jersey and Michigan and then came to Colorado. He got his naturalization papers in Georgetown, Colorado. He worked in the mines in Boulder, Gilpin, Jefferson, Clear Creek, and Lake Counties. He married Mina Ingram on March 1, 1880. Daisy's mother was born in Richland City, Wisconsin, on December 16, 1858, and was living at Silver Plume, Colorado, when she met Albert. They had twelve children. They came to Routt County in 1884 and homesteaded seven miles east of Hayden where they commenced ranching and farming. Mina Squire died March 17. 1904 and Albert then married Martha Watts on October 6, 1905. Albert Squire died on May 15, 1931, in Greeley, Colorado and Martha Squire died on December 19, 1940.

Grandma Daisy Rutherford

Joseph L. Knez

Joe L. Knez was born in Lavinas, Croatia, Austria, March 19, 1890. He came to the United States in 1910 and made his home in Colbran, Colorado with his brother, Mike. Later he took a team of horses and a wagon to Montana where he worked on a ranch. He met Marie (Mahowald) Edwards while at the ranch. They were married July 19, 1914. They moved to Moffat County a few months later, homesteading south of Craig. There he received his citizenship papers.

Joe, a miner at heart, worked at the Walker Mine, and in later years opened and abandoned three mines of his own. He operated the Knez Mine for 23 years. He was more interested in mining than farming, even though it was a very hard life. He opened the Knez Coal Mine which was near the Walker Mine but closer to Craig. He abandoned this mine and opened a new vein of coal a quarter of a mile south in a gulch. This he soon abandoned because a cloud burst filled the gulch and flooded the mine. He began again one quarter mile north and opened another mine higher in the gulch.

This mine was also abandoned and he decided to quit mining and spend more time farming. This only lasted about a year and in 1929, still preferring to mine, he opened another mine that had exceptionally good coal. It was located beside the Knez Divide

Road near the homestead where Antone Knez and his family have lived since the 1950's.

The coal from the Knez Mine was extracted by blasting and pick and shovel. The coal was then loaded onto cars and pulled out of the mine by horses or mules. Later rail track was put down and a cable and winch pulled the cars out of the mine.

Originally he built a cabin near the mines but later he constructed another house located about one half of a mile east of the mine. There still was no running water or electricity. Water was hauled in 50 gallon wooden barrels from the Walker Spring 3 miles away. Rural electricity finally came to the country home in 1948 and Joe built a large tank for water and put in running water and a bathroom in 1949. Natural gas came to Craig a few years later and Joe quit mining. Most people thought coal would become obsolete, but he kept saying, "There will always be demand for coal." He mined there until just before his death. He passed away following a lingering illness. He had two unsuccessful surgeries on his stomach, and died of cancer April 22, 1954.

Joe Knez and His Coal Truck in Front of the Moffat County Court House

Mary (Mahovald) Knez

"Marie" Mahowald was born Mary Mahowald (September 14, 1881) to Mathias Mahowald (born 1833, died 1888) and Mary Sprank in New Market, Minnesota. Mathias was one of five children, all of whom came to the United States from Simmern, Luxembourg in 1852. Mary Mahowald had two sisters: Louise Mahowald Hennes and Margaret Mahowald Braun and four brothers: Matthew, John B., Nicholas P. and Gephard. Mary's first husband was Harry Harry Edwards and of this union a daughter Rosalin was born December 19, 1905. Edwards was a heavy gambler and Mary had to work to help pay the debts. She was a cook in various restaurants. Harry died at an early age from tuberculosis.

After Harry's death, Mary went to Montana where she was hired as a cook at a large ranch. It was there that she met a ranch hand, Joseph Knez, and married him on July 19, 1914. They soon after moved to Craig, Colorado. Joe was hired by Earl VanTassel to work on his farm that winter to feed cattle. He applied for a homestead but had to build a dwelling on the property and fence it in to meet the requirements for getting the title to the land. He began work at the Walker mine and he and Marie lived in a little cabin on the property of the mine. When he was able, he built a small three room dwelling on the homestead land. Louise was born in town on December 8, 1915. Four more children were born of this union: Joseph, Raymond, Marie, and Antone.

Marie Rutherford: I was born November 15, 1920, on my folk's homestead six miles south of Craig, Colorado. I was next to the youngest. I remember how hard people used to have to work to

Miners at the Knez Mine

make a living for their families. When we were small, my mother would go out into the sage brush, service berry brush, and scrub oak taking her children with her. She would clear all this brush off the land by hand with a grub hoe. We would pick it up and put it into piles to be burned later. As they cleared the land, they would plant grain in the cleared areas. My mother kept clearing the brush off the land until they had approximately 360 acres of grain land. We also raised chickens, pigs and cows.

My father also opened a coal mine on the land which was all worked by hand and a couple of horses. All the mining was hard labor and was worked with a pick and a shovel. Carbide lights were used to furnish light for loading coal underground. My father hauled his coal into Craig and sold it to home owners in town for heating and cooking. My mother, during prohibition, would also make bootlegged whiskey and sell enough so we could survive. Dad, afraid of being caught, eventually hid her whiskey-making still so her alcohol producing days ended.

Mount Harris

Yards were large. There were sidewalks. Water was furnished by the mine and electricity, at 50 cents per room per month. The power went off at midnight. Barns were furnished for those who wished to keep a cow. All children who helped clean sidewalks were given tickets to the town movie open on Wednesday and Saturday nights, a different show each time in the show hall. Tickets went for 10 cents each.

Mt. Harris was where the action was, boasting a grand stand two-story bandstand with three bands. There were two baseball teams, one black and one white who played other county teams. Games were hard played, noisy and accompanied by a good amount of under-the-table betting. The ball field was flooded in winter to make a skating rink.

Those who lived in Mt Harris during the good times remember the frame school house that burned and the brick one they built to take its place. They remember the Catholic services held by Father Prinster in the new school gym, Mass, baptisms and communion. Stations of the Cross were observed at the Rutherford house. The Rutherford string band played every Saturday night at the show hall. **Jean Wren, *Steamboat Magazine*, Winter/Spring 1994**

"**MT HARRIS DOOMED** – The once bustling coal town of Mt. Harris soon will be a thing of the past. There are few company towns left anywhere. And mines that do not keep pace with mechanization and modern mining methods cannot be run profitably… There are coal mines today where 60 tons per man employed are produced daily. Mines that bring out only eight or nine tons a day per man cannot justify their existence….

Soon, signs posted around the county announced: "Starting at 10:00 am MST, Tuesday May 20th, the entire facilities and buildings of the Mt. Harris Coal Company, including business buildings, houses, even the bridge, of the entire town will be auctioned …. ALL SALES FINAL EVERYTHING WILL BE SOLD AS IS … WHERE IS! BY THE PIECE, BY THE POUND, WITHOUT LIMIT OR RESERVE." *Steamboat Pilot*, **May 8, 1958**

Mt. Harris Mine and Superintendent's House

Mount Harris Mine, 1912

Mine Bridge and Tipple
1948

Mount Harris with View of Old Wooden Tipple

Part One

BRIGADOON

*Brigadoon, Brigadoon,
Blooming under sable skies.
Brigadoon, Brigadoon,
There my heart forever lies.*

Our Town

Barbara: I was born at a time when the town of Mr. Harris was booming. Coal was necessary for the energy needs of the country. The miners and their families were a mixture of many ethnic backgrounds and everyone together worked hard to make a living in this little mining town I grew to love so much. The employees of Harris Coal lived mostly in the homes on the South side of the tracks. The Wadge Mine Company employees lived on the hill around the elementary school along Highway 40.

Mount Harris Business District ca. 1940s

On the west side of Mt. Harris, between the railroad tracks and the highway, there was a church where the African-American families would gather on Sundays for services. I have no recollection of who the pastor of the congregation was but believe the person was probably someone chosen from those who belonged to the church.

Over time, as the population of the town began to shrink in size, those left were able to move into any housing that was available for rent. By the late fifties, the main concern of the people was the economy of the area and the question on everyone's mind was about future jobs of all who lived there. It was not easy for the miners as they watched the town die little by little.

Uptown

Barbara: The center of Mt. Harris activity was known as "uptown" to us. The stone buildings, all attached, consisted of the Harris Coal Company auditor's office, a retail store (groceries and basic clothing), a drug store/ice cream parlor, barber shop, pool hall and post office.

Dad's job was at the auditor's office. He worked for Otto Hellwig until he retired and then Dad became the head of the office. Susie Taylor was an assistant in the office. It was here that the miner's came to get paid. Payment was often made in company tokens which could then be used in the company stores uptown. This exchange of money for tokens took place at a small entry way at the north end of the office. I would sometimes stop at this little entrance, look over the counter (barely) and ask Dad for a nickel. He would give me two nickels so that I could get two ice cream bars--one for me and one for Marlene.

Tokens and Scrip

On occasion, we would go into his office where we were fascinated by a machine called a "teletype." With this machine, Dad could type messages and send them electronically to the office in Denver. Dad could type very fast even though he used only two fingers to do so. As children, we couldn't go into his office often, but I do remember going with him on occasion after work. He would let us type on a typewriter or watch while he ran the teletype machine. Usually, if we wanted to see him while at work, we would enter a door that was in a small area with a high counter between the customer and Dad. That was the same door where miners picked up scrip to buy things at the company store.

The retail store was where we bought most of the foods that we didn't get through hunting or canning garden produce. I remember the jar of pickled pig's feet sitting on the meat counter at the back of the store. I loved to eat pickled pig's feet when I was a small child. The man who ran the meat section was named Manuel Gonzales and was there until the store closed in 1958. The manager of the store (in the later years) was a man named Harry Scavardi. He came to Mt. Harris from Trinidad and lived in the boarding house. He ate his main meal with us and we got to know him quite well.

Joe Sena and Vic Zullian Main trip, Harris Mine

The drug store was a place to get over-the-counter medicines like aspirin and cold pills. There was also a soda fountain where you could buy malted milks, banana splits, sundaes or just a simple ice cream cone. A very beautiful (in my mind) young lady was in charge of the store. I think her name was Flora Pettry. She was the only child of a woman in the town. The name of the druggist was Mr. Dale Myers.

The barber shop was for the men of the community and had at its entrance the traditional cylinder with red, white and blue stripes spiraling around it.

The pool hall was the gathering place for the drinkers in the town and was totally off limits to us children. Sometimes, we would walk by and peek in but it appeared to be a very dark, foreboding place.

The Post Office was simply that. It was filled with various sizes of mail boxes. Ours was a small narrow one and you accessed the interior by using a built-in combination lock. I knew the combination for the post office box and every day when I walked home from school, I would stop and look into the box to see if we had any mail. On days when we had mail (which wasn't very often--no junk mail in those days), we could see the envelopes through the glass door resting sideways in the box. As I grew, I went from standing on my tip toes to reach the lock to eventually looking straight on into the box.

There was a descending small alley-type road that separated the main building from the dance hall/movie building. This was a large facility that had a dance floor and a kitchen to one side. Community events would happen here and it was in that building that I remember Dad teaching me "Put your little foot..." For a brief time, movies were also shown here.

17

Cars were parked in front of the main building and the road to enter the town was there, too. Across from the building was the home for the doctor and close by was the doctor's office. There seemed to be another building on the west side of the doctor's house but I can't recall what it was. A public pay phone for everyone's use was situated near the doctor's home.

If you continued across the tracks by the main building, you saw a large boarding house where visitors and out-of-town workers could stay if they needed lodging. Early in the life of the town, a cook was hired to provide meals there.

Also on that side of the tracks was the superintendent's two story home and an all-purpose community/hall and church in a beautiful yard. I attended many a wedding and baby shower there with other women and girls of the town. Mrs. Price, the doctor's wife, also used the chapel area for her piano recitals.

Larry: The general store stocked all of our everyday needs. To do some serious shopping, though, we had to go to Steamboat Springs or Craig. When you entered the front door you faced the cashier where you paid cash or used the company scrip. Over to the right was a doorway that went into the drug store/soda fountain. At the left wall was the pay window. The mine office, where Dad worked, was on the other side of that wall. Frequently, when I got out of school I would go the pay window and Dad would give me a nickel to buy some candy. A Baby Ruth bar or Sugar Babies were my favorites. The nickel Baby Ruth candy bar was about the size of the one we pay a dollar for now. Finally, in the back of the store was the butcher shop with a huge wooden chopping block. A layer of sawdust covered the floor.

There weren't any uniformed police in Mt. Harris like Sheriff Taylor in Mayberry. I have read that there was a deputized

Marshal who was one of the miners, however. That was the only official law enforcement in the town. On the other hand, there wasn't much of any crime in the community that I remember either. There was one time, though, when the train depot was broken into and some things were stolen. The thief must have been small because he got in through the little window in the rest room. A teenage boy and I were out in the middle of the street uptown discussing the event when he thought it would be funny to tease me and start accusing me of doing it. Each time he said it he got louder and I got madder. Finally, he was shouting it and I had had enough. I punched him right in the face and gave him a bloody nose. He just stepped back in shock that this skinny little toe-head that was a head shorter than himself would react that way. He could have easily pummeled me into the dust but I guess he decided the fun was over. I really didn't take teasing very well.

I also got annoyed when an adolescent boy would race down from the highway and drive through uptown at what I thought was an unsafe speed. Maybe he would run over one of us kids or our pets. The vigilante in me came out and I schemed how I could end it. I noticed that when he drove across the railroad crossing going into the housing area he cut across at the extreme edge of the crossing. I decided that some nails at that point might nail the culprit. I found some roofing nails that had large heads that I could stand upright at the tracks without anyone else suffering the consequences. It wasn't long that he came roaring through town, once again, and crossed the tracks precisely where I expected him to. He didn't get more than a block or two down the road before he was changing a tire. Justice prevailed!

> I decided that nails at that point might nail the culprit.

Barbara: Dad's salary was about $200 a month the last few years in Mt. Harris. We had to keep our food bill to about $15 a week. We charged everything at the store and Dad paid his bill at the end of the month. Rent was probably about $40 a month at the big house. Gas was $.19 gal. Mom and Dad were able to pay their bills on the little salary he made.

The Mines

Barbara: Harris Coal Company had a very good safety record but that was not the case with the Wadge Mine. When I was very small, Mom and Dad were returning from a trip to Steamboat and, as they approached Mt. Harris, they could hear the sound of emergency mine whistles blowing. They knew there had been some kind of disaster. As it turned out, the Wadge Mine had had a build-up of gas in the interior below ground and there was a terrible explosion. I think that 34 miners were killed. Many families were affected and Mom talked about it for many years.

The Mine Tipple

Larry: The Superintendent's House that we lived in last was about as close as you could get to the actual mining operation. Our yard encompassed our house, the bachelor's quarters and the community church. Just beyond the community church were a series of railroad tracks and the mine tipple. The mine tipple was a structure that stretched over the tracks and railroad cars went under it to be loaded with coal. The coal was brought up from the mine in small rail carts and dumped or tipped (tipple) into a bin where conveyer belts took it up to sorting meshes or screens where extraneous rock was removed and coal separated by size and grade. The coal then went down chutes to fill railroad cars below.

Catwalks ran to various parts of the tipple 2-3 stories above the railroad tracks. It was a fascinating place for 9-11 year old boys. Naturally, we were forbidden to be anywhere near the tipple as it could be very dangerous. But it really wasn't so dangerous when coal wasn't being sorted and loaded, so it seemed to us. Occasionally, we would go up into the tipple and walk around on the catwalks. Once, Uncle Francis, who was the power plant foreman in the building next door, caught us and sent us packing. I don't remember the consequences, but we were sure scared.

Mine Tipple

One time when we were up on the catwalks, probably Johnny Sena, Mike Arroyo and myself, we were taking lumps of coal and throwing them at the pigeons that infested the place. The coal would go crashing against a girder or post and the pigeons would scatter, as pigeons do. One time I got lucky and actually hit one and it spiraled down to the tracks. When we went to check it out we discovered it was only stunned. What luck! I captured myself a pet pigeon. Near the tipple were stacks of rough cut timber that was used for shoring in the mine. In itself, the lumber wasn't that interesting but there were chipmunks that hid between the layers of slats and boards. I thought chipmunks were so cute and believed they would make great pets, so I started stalking them. Sometimes they would get trapped or cornered in the wood but they are really fast and would get away.

Finally, with Eddie's help, I caught one so I took him home and made him part of my menagerie.

Yes, there was much for young boys to do around the mine. There were coal cart tracks and carts far enough away from the mine but near enough to housing for us to push them up and down the tracks without being noticed. We really didn't do that very often, however, because it was forbidden and dangerous.

Nearby, but away from the tipple and tracks, but not far from our garage, there was a "paved" clearing and on the other side were concrete structures which were formerly fuel tank supports. There were three parallel to each other and they had small passageways in the bottom and were scalloped along the top to hold two fuel tanks. We boys imagined this to be the Alamo. We built crude ladders so we could oversee the clearing from above. Then we would take turns being Santa Anna and Col. Travis. Santa Anna's army would attack across the clearing and sometimes they made it and sometimes they didn't. Many battles were fought there and many lives were lost but the fortification probably stands there still.

The Train

Barbara: Train tracks ran through the heart of Mt. Harris. The early trains were powered by steam engines which would stop at

Denver and Rio Grande Steam Locomotive

a water tank just east of the train station to get their fill of water. We became accustomed to the sound of the train whistle as the train came to a stop at the Mt. Harris station.

The tracks were there for both passenger trains and coal-carrying trains. Dad's connection to the train was the mail. He had the job of putting the mail bags from the post office onto the train each evening. I'm not sure he had to get the mail to the train on Saturday nights but, come Sunday night, the mail had to be on the train. That was a problem on occasion because we would have spent the day in Craig and as evening approached, we had to get into the car and head for Mt. Harris. There were times when it became a race with the train to get home. The tracks of the train could be seen from the highway so we would watch the progress of the train from the

> Dad knew that he had to beat the train at some of the railroad crossings if he were to get home in time for his mail run.

interior of the car. Dad knew that he had to beat the train at some of the railroad crossings if he were to get home in time for his mail run. It was a stomach-turner and I'm sure Mom was not happy to be put in the position of racing a train to get home. If we did make it, Dad would jump out of the car, grab the mail bag (provided by Mr. Clifton at the post office) and race to the train station. If it was a close encounter, some employee of the train would reach for the mail bag just as the train was leaving the station. If Dad missed his encounter with the train he had to make the decision whether to return the bag to the post office (not good for his job) or make a dash toward Steamboat to meet the train there.

When Marlene and I were quite young, Mom and Dad decided that we could ride the train to Craig where Grandma and Grandpa were waiting for us. It was an adventure for us and we loved it.

In the 50's, we lived in a two-story house immediately across from the tracks (the Superintendent's House). Ed was a little toddler/child at the time and there were very strict rules about leaving the yard. The gate always had to be locked for his safety. We took those rules seriously because we were told about the dangers of getting onto the tracks. We never knew when a train would be coming.

Coal was loaded into coal cars at the tipple of the mine and then sent out of the town to Denver and the rest of the country. Coal cars were a very familiar sight for us--especially in the booming days of the town.

Larry: The boy's bedroom was upstairs and faced the train depot. Even though the tracks paralleled our driveway, the sound of the train never bothered us. Actually, the train was exciting and fascinating. The railroad tracks ran through town and divided the "uptown" from the housing area. The tracks ran right between our house and the depot with only our driveway separating our property from the tracks. Being right there, so close, it was inevitable that we would spend some time on the tracks. We would walk down the rails balancing as we went. Sometimes we would hop from tie to tie but avoiding ties that had a metal identification button driven into them. Trains didn't come often but they were regular. We boys would take the precaution of putting our ear to the rail from time to time to listen for any trains coming. Sometimes when we knew one was coming we would put pennies on the track to have them flattened. (No nickels; that was big money)

Occasionally, some box cars were parked on a side track in front of our house and they were the homes of some transient railroad workers. The whole family lived in the box car and just traveled along with the work on the railroad. They had small windows and a door with steps that dropped to the ground when parked. That was quite a life.

The Yampa River
Let the rivers clap their hands,
let the mountains sing together for joy; **Psalm 98:8**

Barbara: Rambling or roaring (depending upon the season) along the south side of Mt. Harris was the Yampa River. It was a source of both delight and distress. In the spring when the snow melt was at its peak, the river sometimes became a monster for the town. The water would overflow its banks and the homes along the river's edge were flooded for a week or two. The dirt roads were covered with water and became a muddy mess. I just remember how it affected us when we lived in the "druggist's house" along the railroad tracks. It was there that we had a basement and the water would seep through the foundation and be about ten inches deep. Mom and Dad tried to keep most basement items on high shelves. In order to reach things stored there when the flood would come, we would wear our rubber boots.

When the river flooded, there was always the possibility of

Yampa River

Typhoid Fever so the school children would be lined up at school and taken by bus to the doctor's office to get the Typhoid shot. As far as I remember Floyd Zulian (a couple of years older than I was) was the only person who actually got the disease. He was in the hospital for over a week and we were told that all his hair fell out. I dreaded that three-week series of shots and was the only student who cried from the moment we lined up to get on the bus until the shot was over. I particularly recall the second grade because Miss Rowe pointed out the fact that I was the only one crying. It didn't help the situation.

> **I was the only student who cried from the moment we lined up to get on the bus until the shot was over**

The fun part of the river was the pleasure it provided for fishing, swimming and (in Dad's day) ice skating. The river was fun to be in because the current would carry you along its path. We had rules that kept us from going too far. There were good swimming holes near the Swinging Bridge. I wasn't much of a swimmer but Marlene was a fish. One time when Mom decided to join us under the bridge to watch us swim, Marlene climbed up on the bridge and dived head first into the swimming hole far below. Mom screamed in fear as she saw Marlene make her move, but it didn't do any good trying to stop her. Fortunately, the water was deep enough for the dive. I wasn't nearly as bold and quickly got very cold in the water. I was a bit afraid of leeches, too.

The bridge that spanned the river was known as the Swinging Bridge. If my memory is correct, it was a wooden bridge supported by large cables and concrete supports in the river. It had three "humps" that made it both fun and scary to drive across. It was wide enough for a single lane. Dad didn't drive across it often but, when he did, I was never sure I wanted to be in the car. If you jumped on the bridge, it would wave up and down making it a type of "amusement" ride for us.

Swinging Bridge over the Yampa River

Ed: Dad told me stories about ice skating on the Yampa River that flowed right next to Mt. Harris. He said one time they were skating and one of his friends fell through the ice. He popped up where the ice had broken down stream and climbed out of the river safely and went home. He was very lucky!

Larry: We were never allowed to play down near the river by ourselves but sometimes we kind of wandered away and ended up along the banks. Most of the time the river was picturesque and a place for fishing and swimming. In the spring, however, it scared us. The water was high and near the top of the banks and flowed edge to edge. Although there were no rapids through this stretch of the valley, the water moved ominously fast and threateningly. We boys stayed away then.

Mike, Larry, Ian and James on a Yampa River Canoeing Expedition in 2016

Our Homes in Mt. Harris

The Cinder Block House

Ralph, Marie, Barbara and Marlene Family Portrait

Barbara: As the eldest of four children, I remember living early in the 40's in a little cinder block house that was my "heaven on earth" because of my happy memories there. I had heard later on that Mom and Dad (when first married) lived with Aunt Marie and Uncle Bo in a simple duplex along the Yampa River because there was no housing to be found then--June, 1939. At the time, Dad was working at the US Post Office. He soon acquired a job in the Harris Mine Company accounting department. As soon as housing became available, they moved into their own residence closer to the center of town. It had no indoor plumbing so as soon as the row of "modern" cinder block homes were built, Mom and Dad were lucky enough to be chosen to move in. We were the third house from the west end of town and the Pannell family lived on one side of us. On the other, was the Gene and Jennie Walker family who had three children; the oldest was a boy about a year older than I was -- Genie -- and we played together all the time.

Barbara and Marlene

Our house had five rooms-- kitchen, living room, two bedrooms and a bathroom. There were two enclosed porches, one at the front door and one at the back door. The bathroom and a

Marie and Ralph

large closet separated the two bedrooms. The house was heated by a large coal-powered heater in the living room and the kitchen stove was also powered by coal. I remember how Dad would have to go out in the middle of winter to fill up the coal bucket from the coal house that sat on the alley side of our property. There was an incinerator on each alley side, too, where waste was burned as needed. Every home along the alley had these two small buildings on the house property. It was great to have the coal heat but I also remember the water bottles filled with hot water that Mom so lovingly placed at our feet on those cold winter nights.

I took a nap each afternoon (I wasn't in school yet) and I remember how much Mom read to me from the *Journeys through Bookland* books. Marlene and I would lie down together and Mom would be in the living room. Sometimes we would get up, sneak behind the coal stove in the kitchen to see if she was still there. She was and I suppose she pretended that she didn't know we were trying to find a way to stay up.

Roy Rogers and Mary Hart 1938

Mom would sing aloud while she worked and sometimes had the radio on—KOA from Denver. She liked the Sons of the Pioneers. The songs she sang to us were nursery rhymes and folk songs like *Oh! Suzanna* and *My Old Kentucky Home* and some of Dad's jazz songs. We sometimes got to listen to stories on the radio — Roy Rogers, Gene Autry, and Tarzan.

It was while living at the cinder block house that Larry was born. The house was small but, prior to Larry's birth, Mom and Dad volunteered to host the two Sisters of Loretto nuns who came to teach religion to the young Catholic students in the town. The first two sisters to arrive at our house were

Srs. Placide and Columbiere, Marlene and Barbara's First Communion

31

Sister Columbiere and Sister Placide. We loved those Sisters! The summer Mom was pregnant with Larry, Father Prinster thought it would be too much work for her and decided they should stay with another family. Mom cried.

Larry was born when we lived in that cinder block house. We were beside ourselves with joy when Larry was born. Grandma and Grandpa Rutherford must have taken care of us when Mom went to the hospital because I remember being in front of their house when someone told me that I had a new baby brother. I remember holding him while he was very small and letting him slip off my lap. I was really frightened that I had seriously injured him. We had many, many little cousins and were allowed to hold the newest of them if we could do it correctly. We each begged for a turn at holding any new baby present. This is where we learned about the joy and sacredness of babies.

Mom, Ramona Knez, Edith Fedinic and Barbara

A funny story that I remember is one time when Mom was changing Larry's diaper, I

32

expressed some disgust (it was merely wet). Mom took the diaper and wiped her face telling me that it nothing more than water. I wasn't convinced.

There are a few more thoughts about my life in the cinder block house. Marlene and I shared the second bedroom. I slept in a double bed but Marlene slept in a youth bed which Dad had made for her. She had a problem with potty training so, as a very little girl, would make her bed in the morning if she had had an "accident." It didn't occur to her that everyone knew what had happened the minute we saw the bed. She liked her bed because it had railings along the side (as far as I remember. She might remember more). When she got a bit older, we slept together in the double bed and continued to share sleeping quarters until the day I left for college.

Marlene - 1944

Dad dug a cellar under the house for the storage of canned goods. Mom had a pressure cooker and canned everything from peaches to beans from our garden. We had a modest sized garden in the back yard. There were raspberry bushes in it but very few of the raspberries made it into the house. They were small but delicious. The cellar was all dirt and was a rather scary place to enter but it was required of us to do so to get the food. We didn't question Mom and Dad's commands to help out as needed.

Dad was very helpful in the kitchen when we were young but as we grew older it became the job of Marlene and me to always do the dishes. We took turns washing and drying. I also remember Dad helping with the canning when we were small.

Mom kept the house spic and span and would wash the floor in the kitchen twice a day because coal dust was an ever present issue for the residents of the town. The kitchen and porch floors were covered with linoleum flooring but the rest of the house had beautiful varnished hard wood floors. The walls were all decorated with wallpaper which was not easy to deal with. I remember family members gathering at the house and spending many, many hours cutting the strips of paper to the right length and then laying them on the table with a pan of special paste to get it to adhere to the walls. Once the paper was on for a while, it would get dirty and Mom and Dad cleaned it with a type of "play dough". They would make it into a palm sized oval ball and rub it against the wallpaper. As it got dirty, they would squeeze and twist it until a clean portion of the "dough" could be found. Then the cleaning continued. That was truly hard work.

Barbara, Dad, Larry and Marlene

Mom covered the windows with lace curtains that had to be washed periodically. She would launder them in the wash tubs and then attach them to special curtain stretchers. I loved that job since she would let me put the curtains onto the "nails" that lined the perimeter of the stretchers. It was a fun thing to do.

Barbara Sweeping the Walk

The Druggists House

Barbara: When I was about ten years old, we moved from my much loved cinder block house to a bigger home known as the druggist's house since most of the prior renters of the property had been druggists. The house was two levels. The lower part was a basement that could be accessed from the inside or from the outside. The furnace and storage spaces were located there. The upper level had enclosed front and back porches with windows all around, a kitchen, two bedrooms, a bathroom, and a living/dining room. You reached the upper level by climbing a set of outdoor stairs. It was a wonderful house for us. Ed was born while we lived in this house. His crib was in Mom and Dad's room. Marlene and I shared the other bedroom while Larry slept in a double bed in the enclosed porch. I remember sitting on Larry's bed with Mom one night during a lightning storm. With each flash of lightning, the entire field on the other side of the railroad tracks and across from our house was lit up in a way that you could see well the grassy acreage that was there.

Barbara and Marlene - Easter

I remember being in awe of the entire experience. It was beautiful to behold--God's creation and power all rolled into one. Mom taught us that with each lightning strike we were to say "Lord, have mercy." I haven't forgotten that.

We loved having a baby in the house. Mom did not breast feed very long as was the custom in those days. Formula was encouraged since the doctors thought that to be more nutritional for newborns. I loved helping sterilize the bottles and feeding Ed. I was old enough that I didn't drop him as I had Larry when he was a baby. When I told Mom that I thought Ed was spoiled she responded by saying I was partly responsible for that.

Marlene and Larry

I don't recall too much about living at this house but do remember the spray can of DDT that sat of the window sill of the front porch where our kitchen table was located. The DDT was there to kill flies and other unwelcome bugs that entered our house.

I remember our catechism classes one summer with the Sisters of Loretto. I think they may have stayed with us that year, too, since we fell in love with one named Sister Margaret Ann. She loved to play with us and would get down on the floor for a game of "Jacks." She was very good and we found it was hard to beat her.

While living in this house, Mom volunteered to be the leader of two 4-H classes--the cooking and the sewing. It was great fun and when it came time to make a float for a parade in Hayden, we went all out with chicken wire filled with white and green napkins and crepe paper. I can still see it in my mind today. We rode on the bed of the truck and pretended to stir up some recipes and sew on a machine.

Larry and Ann Rutherford at the druggist house

Larry: The druggist's house had central heating. That is to say it had a furnace in the basement in the middle of the house. There was no duct work. The furnace was coal fired and was automatically fueled by a thermostatically controlled coal stoker. The coal stoker had a large hopper with an auger that fed coal into the furnace when directed by the thermostat. The basement had a coal bin in the corner with a small door to the outside. The delivery trucks would come and dump coal through the door and into the bin. Then the coal would be hand shoveled into the hopper. Frequently, the ashes and "clinkers" had to be shoveled out from below the furnace.

Above the furnace in the living room was an iron grate where the heated air would rise. No one could step on that with bare feet without getting burned. Even though it may not have been convenient, the coal was cheap and the furnace effective. I never felt cold in the house.

The Superintendent's House

Barbara: When I was about 13 years old, we moved in town for the last time into a house known as the Superintendent's House since it had been the home for the superintendent of the mine. It was a wonderful place to live and we felt blessed to have been the ones chosen to live there. The way the allocation of housing worked was, when a house became available, anyone in the camp could apply to live there. The rents were not high because all the housing was owned by Harris Coal, but there were differences in the amount allowed for various houses. Once the application was completed, someone in the company looked over the requests for housing and decided who would be the best tenant. In my mind, I think there were usually about three requests made to move to a vacated house. When we were chosen to move to this last house, we were all elated.

The house itself was large and beautiful inside. It was a two-story home with a partial basement accessed from the interior back porch or from an outside door in the back of the house. All the rooms (except the kitchen and bathrooms) had beautiful hardwood floors--befriended by Marlene and me as we became accustomed to washing, waxing, and polishing them on a regular basis.

On the main floor, there were seven rooms: an enclosed front porch, a reception hall, a living room, an enclosed sunroom, a dining room, a kitchen with a nook, a bedroom and a bathroom. The dining room had built-in china closets in two corners of the room. Glass, French doors were at the entrances of the living room and the dining room from the reception hall. (There may have been French doors between the sunroom and the living room). There were built in book cases in the large living room on each side of an impressive fireplace finished with river rock. It was truly a dream house for us. (Appendix 11)

Crank Handle Telephone

Larry: Just below the staircase in the reception hall was our telephone. It was a very large device that hung on the wall and the case was made of wood. The transmitter or microphone projected from the front and the receiver that you would hold to your ear hung on a "hook" on the side connected by a transmission wire. There were bells on the front that announced an incoming call. A crank was on the opposite side to ring up the operator and to recharge the battery.

To make a call you needed to turn the crank to connect to the operator. She would answer and you would tell her the number

Superintendent's House in winter

you wished to call. At that time most telephones were on a party line. This meant that if you lifted the receiver you could hear the conversation of someone else on that line. It could be very interesting at times.

Barbara: The second story was accessed by a set of stairs that rose from the reception hall on the right as you entered the room. At the top of the stairs, to the right was a very large bathroom with beautiful octagonal black and white ceramic tile and a claw foot bathtub. Larry and Ed's bedroom was to the left of the stairs as you reached the top while Marlene and my bedroom was across the hall on the right. In our bedroom, there was a very small closet that was big enough for all our clothes. We had minimal clothing--all made by Mom. Since we wore dresses and skirts to school, Mom made us a mix and match wardrobe of blouses and skirts. It was the era of crinolines for underskirts and we had three per person--our one seemingly extravagance in clothing. Mom and Dad's room was at the end of the hall and was very large (by the standards of the day). They had a walk-in closet and off to one end of the room there was an entrance to an outdoor balcony. In the summer, Marlene would go to the roof from the balcony or the window in our bedroom to sunbathe. I tried it on occasion but it was way too hot for me.

Eddie and Larry at the Stone Fountain – Superintendent's House

Ed: Marlene and Barbara used to sunbathe on the roof above the kitchen. They would step out of the window of their bedroom onto the roof. One time I went up with them. We were all lying on the roof of the porch sunbathing in the intense sunlight. I was only three or four years old and they forgot I was out there with them. By the time they realized I was out

Larry in Halloween Costume

41

there too long my back was totally sunburned to the point that it was blistered from my neck to my waist. Mom was so angry! I couldn't turn over without considerable pain and she was not happy with the girls because they neglected me.

Barbara: The basement was for storage or for doing laundry. Mom had a double-tub washing machine with a wringer that I loved to use. The laundry went through two tubs for washing and two tubs for rinsing. Dad worked on Saturday mornings so that became the day that Marlene and I concentrated on washing the clothes and cleaning the house. Mom taught us well how to do both of those tasks. We had wire clothes-lines in the back of the house where we hung the clothes in good weather. If it were cold or rainy, Dad had wire clothes-lines hung in the basement. It was a good arrangement.

Eddie and Larry on the Bicycle

It was in this house that Mom and I had a crocheting "contest" one summer. We both loved to crochet so we crocheted decorative pillowcases and scarves for various pieces of furniture in the house. I also put aside some of my work for my "hope chest." It was a very fun thing to do. Mom was good at all things created by her hands and entered her handiwork in the county fair where she garnered many a blue (excellent) ribbon.

Barbara: It was also in this house that we began to see the hand writing on the wall that all was not well with the mine and the coal company. There was very little work for the miners and they were beginning to search for work in other places. Dad, too, knew the time was coming when he would have to find a new job. He and Mom had many conversations about whether they should try to move to Steamboat or to Craig. It was finally decided that Craig would be the better choice since many family members lived there. It was not an easy thing for Dad but, being a rather selfish teenager, I didn't understand all the ramifications of what was going on.

Marlene, Eddie and Larry

Eddie and Larry

As my senior year progressed, the Harris Coal Company decided to close the mine and to sell all the houses of the town. Mom and Dad bought two of them so that they would have lumber to use for the house they hoped to build in Craig. Grandma Knez bought one that was moved to Craig to become her home on Rose Street. Uncle Raymond bought some, too. I remember how Marlene and I helped to take the homes apart by pulling nails out of the boards. I even worked on the top of the roof at one point. It was exceedingly dirty work because the homes had piles of coal dust in the attics. It did pay off, however, because when Uncle Raymond built our home in Craig on the property Dad and Mom bought with some inheritance money Grandma gave them, the cost was reduced considerably. The house had beautiful hard wood floors which were later carpeted.

Dad, Mom, Eddie and Larry

The summer of 1958, Harris Coal Company closed its doors and we moved to Craig. We lived with Grandma Knez for about three months while our home was being built. She was very gracious in having us with her.

School in Mt. Harris

A man shall be known by his learning: but he that is vain and foolish, shall be exposed to contempt. **Proverbs 12:8**

The Grade School

Mount Harris Grade School
Barbara, Marlene and Larry attended here

Barbara: The Mt. Harris Grade School was relatively new when I started first grade. It was a two-story brick structure that was laid out in a manner that put every square foot of the building to good use. Entering the school you climbed a few steps that led to an open area where coat hooks were in evidence and where we left our winter attire (including our winter boots and snow pants). Turning left or right, you encountered staircases that led to the second floor. If you kept going left you arrived at the 1st grade class room (faced south) and the 3rd grade classroom (faced west). Walking down a few stairs, you came to the girls' bathroom at the back of the building. If you turned right, you came to the 2nd grade classroom (faced south) and the 4th grade classroom (faced east). Continuing past the 4th grade classroom, you came to locker rooms and the bathroom for the boys. The classrooms were large and had many windows on the exterior sides of them. On the second floor, there was an open area that served for getting around to the classroom but which had large drapes around it to serve as a stage for school plays and assemblies. To the immediate left of the staircase was another short set of stairs that led to a small Principal's office. Right beyond those stairs was the 5th grade classroom (faced south). Next to it was the 6th grade classroom (faced west). A small descending set of stairs came next which led to the gymnasium. It was here that the entire school would gather for our achievement tests, school plays, sports and community events. If you went right at the top of the staircase, you came to the 8th grade classroom (faced south) and then to the 7th grade classroom (faced east). Another set of small descending stairs also led to the gymnasium.

Mrs. Harder and Mrs. Price

The big Christmas event at the school was the Christmas play. Mrs. Price (wife of Dr. Price) was the music teacher and she went all out with this play. Mom made many costumes for it and they were incredible. The one I remember most included dolls and characters from different countries of the world. There were Italian, Dutch, Spanish and German toy soldiers. We danced and sang and had the best time ever. The older students made up the Christmas chorus for the play. We learned all the old favorite Christmas carols by heart since they were always part of the Christmas program. The community joined the chorus in the singing. It was great! Mom used fabric and crepe paper to make the costumes. We didn't have many pictures taken in those days but I wish we had had some way of remembering those times with pictures. It was at the Christmas program that the employees of the mine received a mesh Christmas stocking filled with an apple, an orange, nuts and Brach's hard candies. It was a wonderful gift for all.

Mt. Harris class of 1950. Marlene Rutherford in the back row

A few words about Mrs. Price. She became our piano teacher after Mom stopped driving us to Steamboat for lessons with Mrs. Gilbert. The Price house, where we took our lessons, was filled with the trophy heads of deer, elk, moose and bear. Dr. Price was a hunter and traveled all over the country to get those prizes. Mrs. Price was a lady to the tee. Dr. Price was, I believe, older than she was, was very short, and quite gruff in manners. It seemed to be an odd match but it worked. She dressed impeccably and wore her hair in an "up do." She was not as demanding a teacher as Mrs. Gilbert but we liked her well enough. One time when we arrived for lessons, we told her that we were sweating. She replied by saying that, "horses sweat, men perspire, and women dew." My girls love that story and laugh whenever I relate it. I have had a mole on my chin all my life and one time when I told her I thought I wanted it to be removed, she told me that it was a beauty spot and I should hang on to it. And so I have.

> She replied by saying that, "horses sweat, men perspire, and women dew."

At the front of the school building was the flagpole and American flag. The upper classmen were in charge of taking it down at the end of the day and putting it up in the morning. Each class day began with the *Pledge of Alliance* to the flag.

Marlene and I walked to and from the school house on the hill. We came home each day for lunch. It seemed that we ate cereal (*Kix* was my favorite) and sandwiches or *Campbell* soup for lunch. Our lunch period was about an hour so we could walk home for lunch. I liked that because Dad would oftentimes join us as he also walked home for lunch. In order to get from home to school, we had to cross the railroad tracks. We took that in stride except for one time when a very long train was stopped on the tracks and a group of us wanted to get home. I was in third grade (I think) but I remember having a long conversation with the other students

RUTHERFORD
2018

48

about how we could best get across the tracks. We could either cross where the cars joined each other or we could crawl under the train. I was scared to death but decided on joining the others who chose to go under the train. I reasoned that if we went at the center of the car we would have a bit of time to get across as the train slowly picked up speed. I don't know if Mom or Dad ever found out about this because I wasn't sure they would have approved.

Mt. Harris cheerleaders; Marlene Rutherford, Beatrice Arroyo, Kathy Montoya, and Patsy Rolando

There were two play areas at the school--one on the west side of the building and one on the east side. The west side play area had swings, monkey bars, and the best-ever merry go round that would be far too dangerous for the "snowflakes" of today. This was an umbrella type merry-go-round that could only work if you hung on by your hands and were about four to five feet off the ground. It was powered by those who pushed it around as fast as they could. If you let go, you fell to the graveled ground and came home with small rocks embedded in your knees, to say nothing about the blisters garnered from this playground equipment and that of the monkey bars. We had a fifteen-minute morning and a fifteen-minute afternoon recess so there was plenty of time to play.

The east side of the building was reserved for baseball, hopscotch, and marbles. When not in use as a playground, it served as a parking area for extracurricular activities.

I was very happy to be able to go to school and was one of the youngest in the class because my birthday fell toward the end of December and the cut-off date for school attendance was the first of January. The first day of school, Aunt Doris (Montieth/Rutherford) brought her little brother George to school. I remember it because he cried. I didn't cry that day but saved my tears for the day Mrs. Murphy put me in the corner because I was talking when I was supposed to be quiet. Mrs. Murphy was a good teacher who helped me fall in love with reading. Dick, Jane, Sally, and Spot became my daily companions in my world of pretend. Mom gave us a good foundation and preparation for reading because she read many stories to us when we were little from the first volume of a children's books (*Journeys Through Bookland*) she had at home. Nursery rhymes, both recited and sung, were part and parcel of our "homeschool" life.

Leonard Rutherford

Larry: She also frequently read short stories of the lives of the saints from small books that I thought were beautifully illustrated. I was very impressed with those stories.

Barbara: The names of my subsequent teachers were: 2nd Grade--Miss Rowe; 3rd Grade--Mrs. Premier; 4th Grade-- Mrs. Harder; 5th

Mom, Dad and Eddie at Mesa Verde National Park 1955

50

Grade--Mrs. Harder; 6th grade--Mrs. Harder; 7th grade--Mr. Hood; 8th grade--Mr. Weinell. My elementary education was solid and there seemed to be no real educational adjustment when the next big step came with the move to Hayden High School. On the other hand, Marlene had a second grade teacher (Mrs. Shreves) who believed children of that age should just have fun. The entire day was a recess for her class and Mom was distressed beyond words about the situation. When Marlene's class entered 3rd grade, the 3rd grade teacher resigned after a couple of weeks because she said she was told that the class had passed to 3rd grade but she had before her a group of 2nd graders. She wasn't prepared to get them up to 4th grade speed in one year.

Mrs. Harder followed my class from 4th through 6th grade. She didn't take any nonsense but seemed to like all of us. Early on, she saw that I was a good speller and decided to tutor me in spelling every day after school in her office (she was also principal of the school at the time). I eventually ended up at the county spelling bee in Steamboat and was the runner-up speller. I still remember the relief I felt at misspelling the word that was my demise because I knew the tension of waiting for the next word would be gone. Mrs. Harder also taught me the importance of following directions when she called me up to her desk after school and told me that I had missed every question on one of the standardized tests we had taken because I did not follow the directions given to us.

Larry: Miss Juchem was my first grade teacher. There wasn't any kindergarten in those days. She was gray haired, almost white, in her fifties and unmarried. I don't remember her smiling much but she could really swing the yardstick if someone needed personal attention. It wasn't so bad though because she only broke it on someone's behind once. My favorite activity in the class was counting and stringing beads.

Uncle Frances and Dad in front of the Grade School

I really thought I was going to get a new teacher when I went into second grade. The school downsized about that time so I was mortified when the first day of second grade, in walked Miss Juchem.

In fifth grade we had Mr. Short as a teacher. He was a stout middle-aged fellow with graying hair and a flat top. He was a bachelor and lived in the teacherage house up the slope from the school. The best part of his class was when he read the classics to us. I remember tears streaming down his face when he was reading *The Yearling*. Another treat was when we got to watch the 16 mm educational movies. It really didn't matter what the subject was, we all enjoyed the break with the half-hour to hour-length films.

A lot of activities in the mining camp took place either at the school or the community church. One year the school put on the play, "The Blue Angel." I don't remember anything about the story but, all the same, it was fabulous. Mom made a lot of the costumes and we practiced regularly during school. It was a musical so everyone got to sing.

Larry: I imagine that the school playground was much like any other at the time. There were the monkey bars, swings, slide, teeter totter, merry-go-round and the "witchs' hat." It might be notable, however, that everything was made of steel and except for the swing seats there was little plastic to be seen. Nor were there wood chips or shredded tires to break a fall. Only plain dirt. At the time the swings seemed to be extremely tall but that didn't stop us from playing "bail out" where we would get as high as we could and then jump from the swing to see who could fly the farthest. Some kids attempted to go around the world and go over the top without falling out. I don't think anyone did it but we did get so high at times that the chains became slack at the top.

The monkey bars and the slide were conventional but had no safety gear anywhere. A merry go round seems pretty innocuous but the kids would get it spinning fast enough that centrifugal force could send them flying if they didn't hold on tightly enough. Then there was the "witch's hat." Here is one creative description of the ride.

The "Witch's Hat" Playground Equipment

> 6th graders would offer to give the younger kids "high rides" lining up a few unsuspecting subjects and invite them to hang on to one end while they would then jam the other right up next to the pole, lifting five or more kids up off the ground. As they began to spin you around it was a thrill for the first minute or so, wind in your hair, legs dangling out from under you as you whirled round and round. Once you realized this ride wasn't going to stop, an icy determination to hang on for dear life took over.
>
> Suspended a good 10 or 15 feet off the ground the bigger kids would spin the ring around the pole, faster and faster, while keeping you, now terrified, high up off the ground. Sweaty palms start to lose grip as your legs swing out almost horizontal from the centrifugal force.
>
> One by one your classmates would fly off, thrown into other playground equipment or even the fence, bodies crumple to the pavement like rag dolls. I can still hear the screams. I survived my high ride and learned lessons about grit, determination, the frailty of life, and the cruelty of mankind. **EVERWAS blog by Ian Kennedy**

I don't think we ever had "snow days" at the Mt. Harris School. If we did, it was rare. Everyone lived within a half a mile or so of the school so all the kids walked to classes. Once you got there no one was allowed into the school until the bell rang. No matter what. My buddies and I arrived at school early one morning but it was snowing and it was bitter cold. We gathered at the front door hoping that someone would have pity on us and let us in. That wasn't going to happen. Since pitiful looks weren't going to work we decided on action. All of us, three or four boys, started kicking the door as hard as we could to get attention. It wasn't long before we did get attention and one of the teachers came to explain that we were in big trouble and she was taking names. We still didn't get in until the bell rang but we did get a RED "D" on our report cards for deportment.

High School

Barbara: I don't remember how many graduated with me from elementary school but, by now the town was noticeably beginning to shrink in size and my class wasn't very big. There was less and less need for coal because other forms of energy were taking its place. Nevertheless, I soon found out that I was on my way to high school.

My high school was a consolidated school made up of young people from Milner, Tow Creek, Mt. Harris, and Hayden. It was located in Hayden, a town seven miles from Mt. Harris. We were bused from our town each morning. Mr. Ed Ulibari was the bus driver when I went off to ninth grade and we all had great respect for him. He had been the bus driver for several years previous to my first ride and would drive the bus to special athletic events. I think we had to be at the bus about eight o'clock in the morning. It would be waiting for us either at the elementary school yard or at the top of the hill along highway 40. It was about a fifteen minute ride to the high school and there were always a couple of "clowns" who acted up on the bus. Our second bus driver was an elderly man (Mr. Wilson) and he would sometimes pull the bus to the side of the road and wait until we became quiet before continuing the trip to Hayden. We were bused home from school about three o'clock in the afternoon.

Dad and Barbara at Graduation ceremony

Marlene – 1956-1957

Our lunch period wasn't very long so we either brought our lunch to school or ate hot lunch in the cafeteria located in the Hayden elementary school. I loved the hot lunches and the two cooks, Mrs. Skufka and Mrs. Ledford, made some of the best food ever. I particularly liked the Apple Crunch and the Cherry Cobbler.

Hayden Union High School Band -- First Row – Marlene Rutherford, 4th from left, Dee Turner (cousin), 2nd from the right and Barbara Rutherford, the right end

It was rather unnerving going from Mt. Harris to Hayden since the high school was much larger than our elementary school and I thought the Hayden students would be a lot more scholarly than we were. That was not the case and the Mt. Harris students did very well when compared with the other students in the class. I was shy, at first, and didn't speak up very often. However, I decided that I would join every activity that was open to me and I loved being a part of these extracurricular clubs, etc. By the time I was a senior, I enjoyed my participation in these activities very much.

The academics were sometimes a challenge for me. I remember particularly one class when I was a junior. Mr. Murphy, my favorite teacher, taught math and convinced me that I should take physics. There were about twenty students in the class and I was one of two girls who signed up for it. After about a week in the class,

> My tears at night when I tried to do the homework didn't soften Mr. Murphy's decision at all.

I decided that it was too much of a challenge for me and I wanted to get out. Mr. Murphy wouldn't let me drop the course and Mom and Dad stood behind him. My tears at night when I tried to do the homework didn't soften Mr. Murphy's decision at all. However, I stayed in the class and did all right for all of my protestations early on to the contrary.

Freshmen girls all took home economics where we learned to sew and cook. The freshmen boys took a class called "shop"

Loretto Heights College

because they learned how to make things out of wood. These were very practical classes at the time and, even though Mom had taught us many of the cooking and sewing skills, I enjoyed taking the class with other girls.

For those who wanted a solid preparation for college, Hayden provided it. I took every class I could that I thought would help me get into college. I liked the challenge that the higher math classes, chemistry, typing, biology, etc. provided. College was a given in our family and I don't really know why because Mom and Dad didn't get an education beyond high school.

When I was a senior, Mr. Murphy tried to convince me to choose Western State in Gunnison as my college of choice since he had graduated from there. Mom had different plans for me, however, and told me that she wanted me to attend a Catholic college for at least one year. Since Loretto Heights was the nearest Catholic college to home, I decided to go there. Leaving home presented a real trial for me because I was so desperately homesick for two solid weeks. I think everyone on the campus knew who I was because I cried uncontrollably wherever I went. Sister Rose Patricia took me under her wing and tried her best to console me to no avail. Time solved the problem and I eventually got to the point that I could attend classes without tears. I made it through the year and by the time the year had come to an end, I had made the decision to enter the Sisters of Loretto in Kentucky--a place far from Colorado. It was the beginning of another stage/chapter in my life.

Barbara at Loretto Heights College

Religion

The fear of God is the beginning of his love: and the beginning of faith is to be fast joined into His love. **Sirach 25:16**

Barbara: We always went to Sunday Mass. There were no exceptions unless you were deathly ill. The only time that I remember I was excused from attending Mass was when I had the flu in high school. Everyone got ready for Mass except me. I knew they would only be gone about two hours but after ten minutes the door opened and in came Mom. She told me she couldn't leave me alone while I was ill so she asked Dad to turn around to bring her back home. She stayed with me and I knew the sacrifice she had made to do it because we all were aware of the love she had for her Eucharistic Lord. She (and Dad) definitely took seriously the third commandment to "keep holy the Lord's Day" which subsequently was deeply ingrained in our practice of the faith, even to the present.

Recitation of the rosary was also a major part of our lives so Marlene and I prayed the rosary together every night. If I fell asleep (as I oftentimes did), she made it a practice to elbow me and listen to me say the second half of the Hail Mary even though she hadn't said the first part. She still likes to tell that story and laugh about it.

There was a Crucifix above the fireplace in the living room of our big house. I was a teen at the time but remember kneeling in the darkened space facing the Crucifix before going to bed and praying my own prayers. I think

> **I was a teen at the time but remember kneeling in the darkened space facing the crucifix and praying.**

Mom and Marlene did the same. It was just a quiet time with Jesus.

Mom's prayers were powerful. She never did like the fact that Dad smoked, but it became more of an issue as she (and he) got older. One night, she said she prayed all night that he would quit. When he woke up the next morning, he was so ill that he was hospitalized and put on oxygen. Mom told God, "I wanted You to break his smoking habit. I didn't ask You to kill him to do it!" Since he was on oxygen, he couldn't smoke. Uncle Francis visited him and told him that this was a good time to break the nicotine habit and quit smoking since he had been forced to give up the cigarettes while he was in the hospital. Dad took the advice and never smoked again.

Father Prinster

Barbara: Dad was a convert to the Faith but we never knew what that meant as children since he was as much a Catholic as Mom had ever been in our eyes. He loved the Church and made sure we were faithful to all of the teachings. We never missed Sunday Mass and had to travel to either Steamboat Springs or Craig to attend these "sacred mysteries" come snow, sleet, or winter blizzard. The parish priest at Steamboat became a regular visitor to our home and a very good friend to our parents. Father Prinster made the arrangements that brought the Sisters of Loretto to stay at our home for a week during

Dad and Fr. Prinster playing the piano

the summer so they could teach the Catholic children of the town the Faith. Father would say Mass about once a month in the school gym for the Catholics in the town. There were very few Anglo Catholics but many Hispanic ones.

As I got older, Father Prinster's visits to our home became more frequent. About once a week, he would call Dad's office to ask him to tell Mom to "put an extra bean in the pot." Father was a very talented musician and played the piano by ear. Dad loved his visits because Father Prinster would sit at the piano with him in the evening and teach him different chord progressions. I was rather selfish during these visits as I looked upon them as more work for Marlene and me. Mom always brought out her finest china and silverware and the evening would be long because we stayed at the table until all conversation ended and then did the dishes by hand.

Fr. Prinster

> Mom told me many years later that she believed someone pushed him to his death.

Father Prinster died one December night when he was trying to remove snow from his roof and slipped to the concrete sidewalk below (Mom told me many years later that she believed someone pushed him to his death. Father had told her that there was a stranger who visited him that he really didn't trust and Mom thought there was some connection). The newspaper boy found his body the next morning. Mom was so very sad and I (in my self-centeredness) didn't see it. She came to the high school that afternoon to pick us up in person, to tell us, and to drive Marlene and me home. I think she just wanted to grieve with someone that day and I didn't understand at the time.

Ed: The first priest I knew was Father Prinster in Steamboat Springs. Father Prinster passed away when he slipped off his roof and fell onto the sidewalk. It knocked him out and then he froze to death. He was found on the sidewalk the next day. After Father Prinster was Father Funk. He told an interesting story about eating poison ivy. He read somewhere or someone told him that if you take a leaf of poison ivy and eat it you will be immune to poison ivy. There was some poison ivy up in the mountains around Steamboat so he found some and picked a leaf and ate it. It almost killed him. They had to take him to the hospital to help him recover.

Sisters Placide and Columbiere

First Communion - A sister of Loretto, Fr. Prinster, Sr. Columbiere and Larry in the back row

Ed: The sisters I remember most were Sister Placide and Sister Columbiere. They were Sisters of Loretto. They taught religious school in the summer and taught at Catholic schools in the winter in Denver. I just loved to be around them because they were very holy women.

Larry: The first time I served Mass was in the Mt. Harris school gym. Fr. Prinster needed an altar boy (in those days you always had to have a server at Mass) and I seemed to be the likely candidate. Maybe it was because when I was little I had an altar set up on the cedar chest in my bedroom and would periodically say Mass there. Or maybe it was because I dressed up like a bishop when we were living in the druggist's house.

In any case, I was to be the one that morning but I really didn't have a clue what to do. Father figured he would coach me along during Mass but I didn't want to be up in front of everyone not knowing what I was supposed to do. I had tears streaming down my face all during Mass as I suffered the pain of embarrassment.

Bishop Lawrence

Larry's Altar in the Bedroom

Home and Family

Clothing and Fashion
Strength and beauty are her clothing, and she shall find joy in the times to come. **Proverbs 31:25**

Barbara: Growing up, Marlene and I didn't have a lot of clothes. It wasn't necessary and we didn't have the space in the closet to store them anyway. Mom made our clothes and we were happy that she did. She made mix-and-match skirts and blouses. She bought some cardigan sweaters to go with the skirts. I loved my simple high school wardrobe.

When we were very young, the women and girls of the family wore dresses or skirts -- no pants unless we were going to the hills. Our grandmothers wore dresses all the time (no matter the occasion) and wore aprons in the kitchen. I think Grandma Daisy wore an apron to picnics. It was just part of her attire. Our skirts were mid-calf. In the high school, the girls wore skirts but introduced the custom of wearing jeans on Fridays (game days). It was a strange practice,

Marlene and Barbara in Prom Dresses

looking back, because the athletes dressed in nicer clothes on game days while the girls dressed in jeans.

For the prom, strapless gowns with poofy nylon net and ankle length skirts were the rage, but Mom wouldn't allow us to be like everyone else. She made our prom dresses and made them with straps. Modesty was extremely important to her. The dresses were always very beautiful although I would always find something wrong with them. I wasn't the best natured teen on the block those days. Looking back, I should have been exceedingly grateful at the time for all that she did for us. She was an excellent seamstress and could merely look at a picture of a dress and make it up--often within the course of a single day. How wonderful was that?

> She made our prom dresses and made them with straps. Modesty was extremely important to her.

Ed: I remember the sun suits Mom used to make for me. They were little sun outfits with shoulder straps, open on the sides and shorts. I don't know why but I liked those clothes so much that they were what I preferred to wear. It was interesting because once we moved to Craig that was the end of the sun suit. I never wore them again and I really missed them. Things changed suddenly and I didn't really understand why.

Larry: Mom made a lot of our clothing. She was an expert seamstress and even made me trousers at one time. I remember a sailor suit she made for me from Uncle Leonard's

Larry in Sailor Suit

sailor's uniform. How she was able to make a kid's suit out of an adult uniform was quite amazing.

She wasn't able to make all our clothes, however, and every summer we would get out the *Montgomery Ward Catalogue* and order all the basics for school. In the fall, the order would arrive in a big box or two and they would be filled with lots of gray paper bags with the clothes for the school year. It was almost like Christmas opening that box.

Barbara: When we were small, Mom took great delight in curling my and Marlene's hair. In those days, bobby pins were the best means of making curls in little girls' hair and Mom made good use of them. The two of us were born with naturally very straight, blond hair. Mom was meticulous in the care of her own hair and saw to it that we, also, had an elegant head of curls.

As we got older, Mom began to use permanents to insure that we had our curls. She became an expert at giving them to us and we regularly sat before her as she began the hour-long process of applying curling chemicals to our hair. As a youngster, I thought the "permanent" curls were wonderful so didn't mind the process involved to get them. When I became a teen, I was much more critical of the results but would still agree to be subject to the perming action on condition that the end result would not be a "frizz." I still remember being quite jealous of two teenagers who were two years older than I was--Glenda Tabb

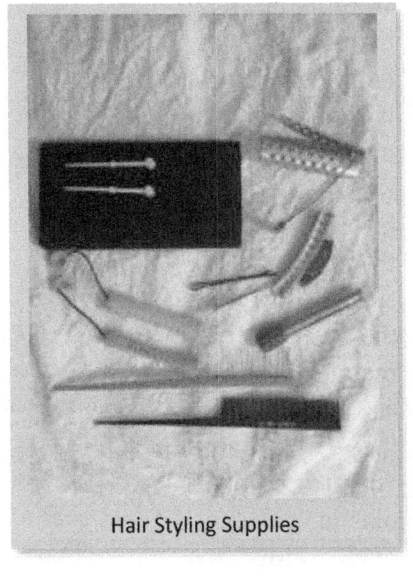

Hair Styling Supplies

Barbara with a Permanent

and Kathleen Frentris. Both had wonderful, natural curly hair that was worn short in a "duck tail" cut. (It was a common hair style of the 50's.) Their hair was always perfectly groomed and didn't vary from tight curls to loose curls as mine did, depending upon the rollers used to achieve the desired results. I was like Charlie Brown in the sense that I would look forward to the perm knowing that THIS TIME my hair would be just like Glenda Tabb's and each time, when Mom took out the rollers, I would look at myself in the mirror and say "not yet." Mom was so good to keep trying to please me.

Without perms, I had to curl my hair every night with rollers that made all girls look like they had just arrived from outer space. Early on, they were large, metal rollers but, as time passed, they became very colorful plastic ones. How we

Barbara and Edie Fedinic with Roller Curls

went to sleep on them, I do not know. Marlene and I would wash our hair often and spend each night rolling up our hair on those curlers. The results were not all that bad considering that our hair had no sign of curl in it before.

I continued to give perms to myself until I reached my seventies. Those "false" curls made hair care so easy but I began to tire of the time and effort it took to have easy-care hair. Straight hair is now the acceptable hair style for me. I have decided with St. Peter that "Your beauty should consist of your true inner self..." (I Pet. 3:4). Hopefully, that inner beauty can shine forth a bit because the hair beauty disappears with time. It is not a bad thing.

Entertainment

My parents had us very young. We lived in a modest house. We built forts, we hiked, we went camping and they wanted us to be independent. It's how children grew up in the 1940s and 50s: outside all the time, playing in the dirt, riding your bike around. **Auhor Brooklyn Decker**

Barbara: Dad worked five and a half days each week. Sunday was always reserved for Church and fun with family. We spent it either around Steamboat (Fish Creek Falls/Hahn's Peak) or with the Knez families in Craig. It was great being young in those days.

In the winter, we would go sledding off the hill between the school and the tracks. In the summer we played kick the can, especially when visiting our cousins at night.

We had no television but did listen to the radio. Every morning Mom would listen to the music of the Sons of the Pioneers, a western group. I still remember the song "Drifting Along with the Tumbling Tumble Weeds." As children we became fans of the Gene Autry and the Roy Rogers programs. We huddled around the radio on the floor to hear them because reception was not always that good. She also listened to KOA news and two items that I remember from my childhood was the execution of the spy couple, the Rosenbergs, and the coronation of Queen Elizabeth II. Somewhere along the way, I heard that "England left the Church under Elizabeth I and would return under Elizabeth II." It is rather late (it seems) for that to happen and no one in recent memory has ever heard of this "prediction." Was it just

Listening to the Radio

the wishful thinking of a little girl? I guess I won't know that answer any time soon.

We did have a phonograph and Mom bought a record collection of the *Life of Christ* that we loved to listen to.

The radio was also part of the Rutherford love of the sport of boxing. I grew up hearing about Rocky Marciano and Joe Lewis because the Rutherford brothers would gather at Grandma and Grandpa's house and, sitting close to the radio, listen to each and every blow that would fall on the boxers. Those were some of the few occasions that we were invited to Grandma and Grandpa's home since Grandma, in particular, was rather distant--especially to children. Whenever we went there, we did very little talking and sat quietly on the couch or chair listening to the adults. Once, Grandma offered us some cookies she bought at the store. We thought they were the best cookies ever because the cookies at home were always homemade by Mom. How little we knew about quality!

Larry: Television didn't come to the Yampa Valley until after we got to Craig. We had a little portable TV that was on a roll-around stand. It had "rabbit ear" antennas that you frequently moved this way and that to help make the very poor black and white picture a bit better. We only had TV at all because they put a repeating transmitter on the top of Rabbit Ears Pass. Although the picture gradually got better over the years, it contained varying intensities of "snow" that nearly obliterated the picture.

Still, we would gather around the TV frequently for dinner, eating on our TV trays and watching programs like *"The Carol Burnett Show"*, *"Bonanza"*, *"The Dick Van Dyke Show"* and *"The Andy Griffith Show."* It was all pretty harmless but addictive all the same.

Larry: We had lots of group outdoor games which were important when all the family got together. One of the favorites was *Red Rover* where two equal lines were formed by kids holding hands and facing each other. The leader would call out "red rover, red rover send (name) over," with his team's consent, which person on the other side was challenged to run across as fast as possible and try to break through the opponent's line. If the person failed they would join their opponent's team. If he was successful a person where the breakthrough occurred was taken back to the challenged team. The play continued until there was only one person left on a team.

While us boys played marbles all the time and kept a bag of marbles in our pocket so we would be ready to play anytime, the girls played jacks and hopscotch.

Boys Playing Marbles

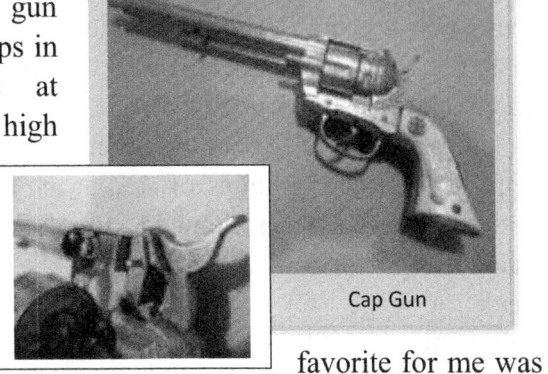

They would draw a hopscotch pattern on the sidewalks with chalk and compete among themselves.

No one thought too much about guns at school. Students, and probably teachers too, had rifles in the gun racks in their pickups in the parking lots at school. In junior high the boys brought cap guns to school to play with before classes and at recess. The favorite for me was a two shot derringer type that had authentic looking bullets with caps inside. Cap guns were toy pistols that you would load with a roll of paper that had a small spot of gunpowder in it that popped when the hammer of the pistol hit it. It automatically advanced for multiple gunshots. Some had realistic bullets with caps that you could load into a revolving cylinder.

Barbara: As I have said before, we had no TV or social media to keep us entertained. We played board games like *Clue*, *Monopoly,* and *Checkers*. We loved jacks and jumping rope. Mom and Dad played card games with their friends and taught me to play *Canasta* at a young age. I loved that game and played it with anyone who would give me an hour of their time.

Larry: When we lived in the Superintendent's House we had quite a few pets. First of all, we had two dogs; Koko was a collie mix and Lady was small like a sheep dog. I was fascinated with wild animals as well. Near the mine tipple there was lumber stacked for use in the mine. There were a lot of chipmunks living between the slats and I decided I was going to catch one. With the help of Eddie, I was able to capture one. It was not a happy chipmunk and it tried to bite me all the way home. We caught a pigeon, too, by going up into the catwalks of the mine tipple and throwing lumps of coal at the pigeons. We hit one and it fell to the ground stunned. I took it home and Dad and I made a cage for it. We made a cage for the chipmunk as well but it never stopped trying to gnaw its way out. Someone, I think it was one of our cousins, gave us a baby owl. It was put in a large cage but it was never tamed. We would feed it raw meat and when we approached the cage it would fly at us with its talons in the attack position. Inside, we had parakeets from time to time. Eventually we had to free all the wild animals. The chipmunks and the owl were gone in short order but the pigeon kept returning as long as we fed it.

Pet Owl

Ed: Mom and we kids really liked Mt. Harris. We made up many kinds of games. There was a structure with one big concrete wall that, in our imagination, looked like The Alamo. So we devised our own "Remember the Alamo" game. Of course there were the attackers on the outside and the Texans on the inside defending the place. I also went with my brother Larry to this stack of railroad ties in the area that had a really stinky smell of creosote. He put a pair of leather gloves on and hunted for chipmunks in the pile. I would get at one end of the stack and when we'd see a chipmunk I would chase it and the chipmunk would go down the railroad ties and run down underneath them. Then he would pop out on the other side and Larry would grab him with the leather gloves he had on his hands so they wouldn't bite him. Afterwards, we took them back to the house and put them in a cage.

We also had two dogs, Koko and Lady. Koko was a collie and Lady was a cocker spaniel. They were beautiful dogs, fun companions and good friends. But there came the time when we had to move to Craig. Dad loaded them up in the car to find a home for them. I asked if I could go and I went with him to the farm where he gave them to the farmer. I cried all the way home.

Larry: My friends were a picture of diversity. Kent Franz and I were the token Anglos and Mike Arroyo, Tink Arroyo, Johnny Sena and Freddie Santistevan were our Hispanic representatives, Frankie Wilson was African American and Anthony Angelo, I believe, was Italian. We didn't think about these differences that much. We just played together. I don't actually recall everything we did while we were out and about. Sometimes in the morning I would go down to the Arroyo's and Mrs. Arroyo would be making tortillas in the kitchen on their coal fired kitchen stove. You could smell their wonderful aroma as you approached the house. If I was lucky, she would give me

Johnny Sena, Isidro Arroyo, Larry Rutherford, Mike Arroyo, and Eddie

a delicious treat of a tortilla rolled with thick whipping cream and jam inside.

We really liked going to the movies, but I don't remember attending many movies while we lived in Mt. Harris. It was too much of a trip to get to the Chief Theater in Steamboat Springs or to the West Theater in Craig for us to go often.

The movies were pretty simple, then in one way, but lots more complicated in other ways. There was a lot more dialog in the script, and, I believe more story telling. Probably it would be pretty boring for the contemporary audiences. The earlier movies were in black and white but the full color movies became more common after 1940. *The Wizard of Oz* (1939), *Gone with the Wind* (1939) and *Fantasia* (1940) were some of the most notable pioneers in color.

When we moved to Craig, it was very easy to get to the theater. The West Theater was only 4-5 blocks away and the movies were a great pastime. We even had an outdoor "drive-in" theater with the tinny sounding speakers on a post that you parked next to and hung on

Abandoned Drive-in Theater

your car window. Refreshments and restrooms were a hike to the back of the parking area below the projection booth. Sometimes people would just sit outside on the tailgates of the pickup or station wagon. Nearly all have faded into history.

There were the epic movies made with few "special effects" and no CGIs, needless to say. Directors of these movies, many times, had to orchestrate and choreograph complicated live-action scenes with thousands of actors ("extras"). *Land of the*

Pharaohs (1955) and *Spartacus* (1960) had over 10,000 extras. The Ten Commandments (1956), *Ben Hur* and *Fall of the Roman Empire* (1964) are still awe-inspiring both for performances and monumental filmmaking. *Dr. Zhivago* (1965) is noted for the beautiful score and breathtaking cinematography.

Another innovation that has come and gone is the wide screen *Cinerama* technique that originally projected images simultaneously from three synchronized 35 mm projectors onto a huge, deeply curved screen; a 146 degree arc. The audience being "enveloped" in the screen felt like they were part of the movie itself. Because of the cost and technical complications the huge movie screens were largely abandoned.

I would not say that all the movies of the 40's, 50's and 60's were great. They were not. But even the silly, trite, banal, poorly acted and cheaply made were mostly harmless and with a low bar entertainment level. There were *Beach Party* (1963), *Gidget* (1959), *Tammy and the Bachelor* (1957) and dozens more. I say most were harmless since merely the line by Clark Gable in *Gone with the Wind*, "Frankly, my dear, I don't give a damn" caused a scandal and an uproar. That wouldn't even cause a blink of the eye today.

> "Frankly, my dear, I don't give a damn" caused a scandal and an uproar.

Another unique thing about the movies of the time was the Catholic Legion of Decency which was formed in 1933 to combat objectionable content in movies. Even after being approved by the secular offices of Hollywood's Production Code, the movie would be sent to the Legion of Decency before being released to the general public. Condemnation by the L of D could shake the core of the movie's success because Catholics, 20 million strong at the time, would be prohibited from viewing the movie under pain of mortal sin. A pledge to support the Legion of Decency was recited after Mass and at some parishes it was a signed pledge.

The rating system was as follows:

- A: Morally unobjectionable
- B: Morally objectionable in part
- C: Condemned by the Legion of Decency

The A rating was subsequently divided:

- A-I: Suitable for all audiences
- A-II: Suitable for adults; later — after the introduction of A-III — suitable for adults and adolescents
- A-III: Suitable for adults only
- A-IV: For adults with reservations

In 1978, the B and C ratings were combined into a new O rating for "morally offensive" films.

Our family followed these ratings and did not attend any B or C rated movies, period. The Legion was later absorbed into the United States Catholic Conference and subsequently into the United States Conference of Catholic Bishops. The rating systems and reviews have been largely ignored by the Catholic population since the 1970's and have currently faded into the woodwork of the Catholic News Service. Here is a book listing the ratings of all movies between 1933 and 1959 if you would like to see what the LOD ratings were like:
https://archive.org/details/motionpicturescl00nati

Back in the 1950's Aunt Cleo and Uncle Antone almost never went to a movie. One night Uncle Antone thought that they ought to go out to watch a movie at the theater. They didn't really know what was playing, but in those days it was a pretty safe bet that it would be OK. Well, the movie playing was *Underwater* (1954-1955) starring Jane Russell. They left the movie stunned and outraged at what they saw. They found out later that it was "B" rated. The LOD objection was "suggestive costuming and situations."

Jane Russell in *Underwater*

Food and Hospitality

Do not forget to show hospitality to strangers, for by so doing some people have shown hospitality to angels without knowing it.
Hebrews 13:2

Barbara: Mom and Dad loved to have dinners at their home—something that Dad loved till the day he died. They seemed to like everyone in those days. Did they ever hold a grudge against anyone? I can't remember that they did. Any hurts were quickly forgotten and forgiven from my point of view as a youngster.

There were wonderful cooks in our family but, I have to admit, I think Mom was the best. For ordinary days, we had a standard meal of meat (mostly wild game), mashed potatoes, white gravy and some vegetable. Desserts were for holidays or occasions when we were hosting guests. Where Mom excelled was in cooking for guests, whether family or friends. She seemed to love to cook and made the best ever breads and desserts.

Hunting and fishing were sports for the men in the family but were also great sources of food for everyone. Since the men hunted deer and elk to keep the freezers full, it was not uncommon for the game to be obtained out of season. Many a time we were instructed to refrain from saying anything to anyone about the deer or elk hanging in the garage on the farm. It didn't seem at all odd for us at the time. It was just a way of life.

One of my favorite breakfast items as a child was hot milk and toast. I must have stopped eating it somewhere on my way to becoming a teen, but it was a delicious item for me when we lived in the cinder block house. I always put lots of butter on the toast and it would melt in the hot milk in the bowl. I wonder if anyone eats it today?

Dad was a real fan of Mom's cooking and he enjoyed eating it as much as she enjoyed cooking it. Dad, himself, did very little cooking but he was an expert in making pancakes. I think everyone remembers well the breakfasts he cooked when we would arrive as guests at 789 Tucker Street. He also loved ice cream and always had a stash of it in the freezer for the grandchildren.

Grandma Knez would cook many a chicken dinner for us -- chicken and dumplings were a favorite. It was not uncommon for us to watch as she slaughtered the chicken in the morning knowing it would be eaten later in the day. She made sauerkraut and cottage cheese in large glass vats that rested in her kitchen. Her German background was in evidence then.

Spam Canned Meat

Grandma Rutherford made fried chicken her specialty and although I have but one memory of eating it at her house, the family knew she was an expert in this field. Grandpa Coke's favorite breakfast was bacon and eggs and I think he ate it every day until the day he died.

Larry: As I remember, we also had sliced canned Spam fried for breakfast. Spam's basic ingredients are pork, with ham meat added, salt, water, modified potato starch as a binder, sugar, and sodium nitrite as a preservative. It was served frequently to American soldiers during World War II and had various affectionate nicknames. Mom also made her own noodles and served them in a kind of chicken gravy over mashed potatoes. Oysters were part of our diet from time to time and served as oyster chowder or breaded and fried. Although I ate them without complaining, they had some very chewy parts and they retained some of the sea sand which didn't add to their palatability.

Mom was not only a welcoming hostess and a great cook, she loved to set a beautiful table. Even though both Mom and Dad came from humble mining and farming backgrounds, growing up in a coal mining camp and a rural homestead in the country, they understood beauty, manners and etiquette. The table was set formally to honor guests and not for show. There were china plates with beautiful yellow roses on them, lovely polished silver-plate tableware set with each piece in order. How could she know these things and why did she do it this way? It was in her nature and she did it for a love of beauty and a love of people.

> It was in her nature and she did it for a love of beauty and a love of people.

Barbara: Mom and Dad were always welcoming to strangers. I saw that first when they opened the house to the Sisters of Loretto. I wasn't around when Mom really opened the doors but Dad told me that he couldn't begin to count the number of strangers who set foot in and stayed in their home. If she saw a new face at church, she would immediately approach the person and ask if they had a place to stay. If the answer was "no", Mom would invite them to come to 789 Tucker since there seemed to always be room there.

Barbara, Eddie, Marlene, Dad, Larry and Mom
1959

Once I left home, I never hesitated bringing friends home with me since I knew the welcome mat would be out for them. She was also compassionate. When I was little, Mom and Dad often picked up strangers on their way to or from Steamboat. It was a safe thing to do back then. But, as time went on, there were enough tragic hitchhiking stories that they stopped the practice. That is, however, until we were on our way to Larry and Fran's wedding in 1970 and had reached Washington, D.C. There was a young man dressed in a military uniform who was hitchhiking along the entrance ramp. It was cold and snowy--a January evening. We drove past him (I was driving) when Mom said she wanted to turn around and pick him up. She told us that, if he were her son, she would hope someone would give him a ride. Ed and Mom were in the back so Dad (who had many reservations about it) said he would consider it even if there was risk involved. Dad said he would ride in the back behind the soldier so he could keep an eye on him. We did turn around and stop to pick him up. We didn't know where he was going but he gave directions to his destination. When we got to the Gastellum home, Louie told Dad that we had gone a long way out of the way to accomplish our goal.

> We drove past him when Mom said she wanted to turn around and pick him up.

Ed: Mom entertained guests so well and was such a gracious hostess. The Sisters of Loretto would come for a couple of weeks in the summer and teach a religious school at different parishes. When they were in Steamboat they would come down to the house and she would make them a marvelous dinner. She would bake her own dinner rolls and cook everything from scratch. I remember going up to Father Prinster's for dinner and he said, "Eddie, did you wash your hands." "I wash em, Favvy." Everyone thought that was very funny.

Larry: An activity we frequently enjoyed in the fall of the year was picking chokecherries. Chokecherries are found in many areas around Northwestern Colorado and we even harvested them along the road near Grandma and Grandpa Knez's house. They are called chokecherries for a reason. They are very sour even when ripe but that didn't keep us kids from eating a lot of what we would pick. We would all be given tin cans and we would climb up into the bushes with large trunks and gather the cherries to combine in large buckets to take home. Mom always canned chokecherry jelly which is my favorite, even yet.

Health and Illness

Honor the physician for the need thou hast of him: for the most High hath created him. For all healing is from God, and he shall receive gifts of the king. Sirach 38:1-2

Barbara: Mom seemed to have medical problems (especially with her back) but she was always very happy and would joke and tease us. I learned that her back problems were the result of a fall she had taken off a horse when she was high school age. She went to see chiropractors quite often. On occasion, she would travel to Denver to see good chiropractors and Dad would have to find help from his family to care for us. These were always unhappy times for me and I would cry because I missed Mom and it always seemed that no one really wanted us to be with them.

Larry was about two years old when he drank some *Clorox* which was sitting on the sink when Mom was washing clothes. He passed out and Mom ran screaming down the alley "My baby is dead, my baby is dead." Jenny Walker drove her uptown to the doctor's office where Larry recovered. It was rather traumatic for me.

> Mom ran screaming down the alley, "My baby is dead. My baby is dead."

The doctors who I remember were Dr. Ligon Price and Dr. Bassinger. They were employed by the union and I think there was a nominal fee for each visit. In those days, you visited a doctor only when necessary. There was no such thing as a well visit. When I was about nine years old, I was riding my bike down the alley when a piece of burning paper flew out of an incinerator and burned my leg. Soon after, I began breaking out with boils on my leg. It was thought that the ink of the paper poisoned my blood. Mom tried to treat the boils herself by opening and draining them but the process was unsuccessful and I would end up by having to go to the doctor to have them lanced. Most times this was done in the office but I still remember Dr. Price coming to the house to do the procedure. I am sure that everyone within the area heard my screaming in protest. This was very hard on Mom and Dad since Dad, in his kindness, would drive me to school. I took a pillow with me because it was painful for me to sit on the upper leg boils. But I didn't want to miss any days at school.

Hayden had the nearest hospital and it was there that the Mt. Harris doctors did surgery and birthed new babies. It was a two-level hospital and still stands today as a clinic/hospital on the hill overlooking downtown Hayden. Steamboat also had a hospital and it was there that I was born. Dr. Crawford was Mom's obstetrics doctor.

Larry: I contracted mumps while we were living in the Superintendent's House. I was quarantined to the cook's bedroom off the kitchen and all the shades were drawn. Light sensitivity is part of the disease, so the room had to be kept dark. Doctors still made house calls so Dr. Price came to see me every day. He lived just across the railroad tracks so it wasn't very hard to do.

The Yampa River would overflow in the spring many times and flood the residential areas of the town. Since there were still some homes with outdoor toilets and cesspools the water would get contaminated. This meant that everyone in the community would have to get typhoid shots. It certainly was dreaded by all us kids but it had to be done. Later, there were levies raised along the river banks to prevent the flooding.

Barbara: Sometimes, the Yampa River would overflow and flood the town. On occasion, typhoid fever would break out and the school children would all be taken to the doctor's office to begin the series of three shots. Even when the school children didn't go *en masse*, Mom would make sure we received the shots because she was very concerned about our health. I hated any kind of shot and was the only one in second grade to cry when I stood in line to get it.

Yampa River Flood

Larry: We didn't go to the dentist very often, as I recall, maybe once a year to get teeth cleaned and to fill cavities. There was no fluoride in the water or in the toothpaste. There was no dental floss. It seems to me that every time I went to the dentist I had to have one cavity or more filled.

We went to Steamboat Springs to visit the dentist. The dentist's office was very simple. No doubt there was more there but all I remember is "the chair." X-rays were taken but they had to be developed because there were no instant pictures then. Maybe there was a dental assistant, but I only remember the dentist. You got up into the chair but it did not recline much, if any. On the left was a spit bowl with a small stream of water swirling around inside. That was used when you were to spit out fragments or material from the dental process. The grinding of a cavity seemed interminable. Then it was filled with a silver-colored mercury "amalgam" which is mercury mixed, about 50/50, with a combination of silver, tin, copper and other metals. That was pressed into the cavity and you spit out any extraneous particles. It was not the most pleasant experience.

When I was in college, I had a cavity with a serious flare up of pain. I had to go to the dentist which was not high on my list of fun things to do. I also hated needles. I went in and when the dentist was about to give me a shot of Novocain, I declined. (I guess I imagined that drilling would be less painful than a couple of needle pricks.) He proceeded to drill and drill deeper and deeper inflicting excruciating pain. Finally, I passed out so he had to revive me, give me a shot and proceed. That was a lesson. I learned the value of Novocain.

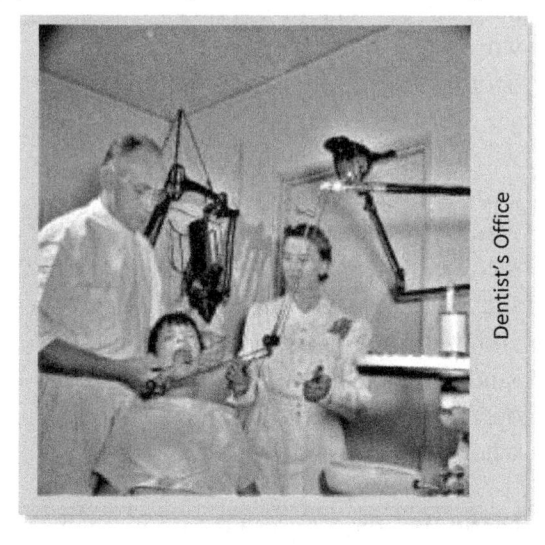

Barbara: Mom had grown up knowing firsthand what it was to have childhood diseases. A very distinct memory for her was that of having whooping cough and thinking she would die because she couldn't get her breath. Grandma Knez told about diphtheria and the ravages it had on the population in her days. There were no immunizations of the diseases then so, when shots appeared on the scene, Mom was at the front of the line getting them for us. If I remember correctly, we only got shots for whooping cough, tetanus, small pox and typhoid fever. There were no measles or chicken pox immunizations available. The small pox scar from the immunization is still slightly visible on my upper arm. No one gets the small pox immunization today because it has, apparently, been eliminated from the world.

I remember the morning I woke up with a very sore jaw but didn't want to tell Mom because I loved school and didn't want to miss a single day. However, by the time I had eaten breakfast I knew I had to mention it because mumps was making its way around the school. Mom did keep me home and I endured the course of the disease on one side of my face. I don't know why it didn't affect both sides of my jaw. I think Marlene escaped getting the disease.

Marlene and I both had measles at the same time and I remember Mom keeping the house very dark during the day because there was some evidence that the disease could affect our eyesight. I

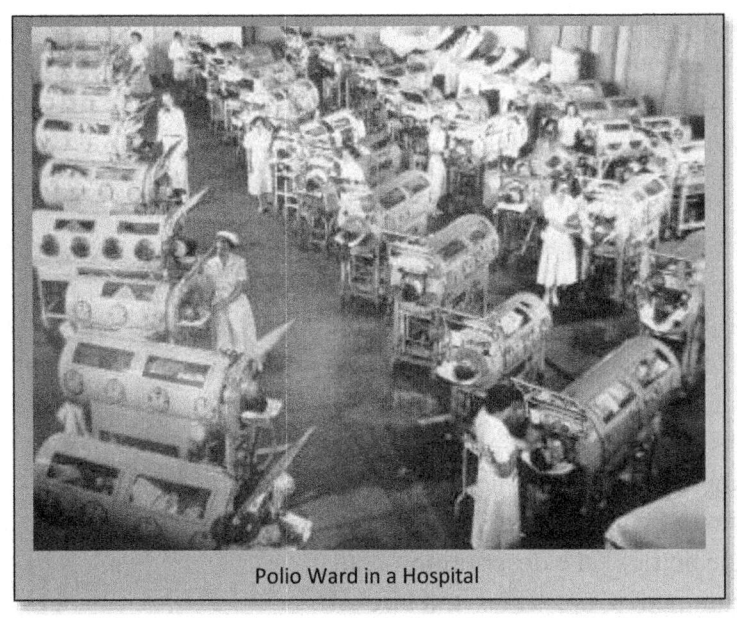

Polio Ward in a Hospital

don't recall whether it was the 3-day measles or the red measles. One was supposedly worse than the other. It was sometimes fatal. The big scare for disease came when polio made its appearance in our country. All water activities (like running through the sprinklers) were out of the question because no one seemed to know the cause of the disease and some were saying it was caused from contaminated water. I was probably about ten years old at the time. Then, the miracle drug was discovered by Jonas Salk and the vaccine became available when I was about 15. Mom, who rarely came to the high school after classes, appeared out of nowhere with the instructions that we were on our way to the doctor's office for our shot. How I hated any shots but I knew it was fruitless to try to get out of this one. Polio was a killer and crippler disease and many who got it ended up in an iron lung fighting for life. The vaccine was a blessing.

Colds and flus were not uncommon. There was a little black pill that tasted like pressed coal dust (as if I knew what that would taste like) but it was a regular remedy for colds. Mom would also make us a hot toddy with lemon, honey and a bit of whiskey. When Dad tried to make this same remedy for Uncle Francis' flu, Uncle Francis (who never touched liquor) said he would rather die than drink that stuff.

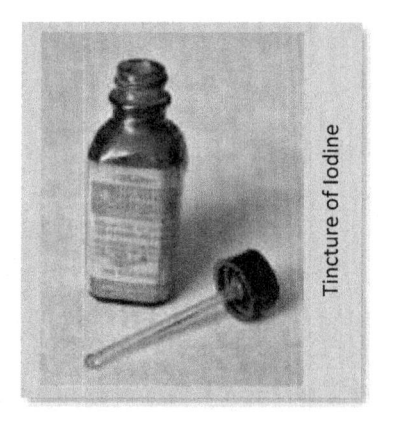

Larry: There were other common first aid remedies and medicines found at home. Tincture of Iodine, Mercurochrome and Merthiolate were used as antiseptics and all burned like the dickens. The idea was that you applied these red liquids to the wound with a glass rod dipped in the bottle. One description I read summed it up, "This tincture of hellfire with a glass rod served as a hot poker to apply battery acid to the wound." You could be satisfied it could kill anything it touched. It also left a yellow/red stain on the skin as additional proof that it worked.

Castor oil was administered as a laxative. If that didn't work there was the diabolical enema tube with the rubber water bottle. You always hoped the castor oil worked.

When we had colds or coughs Mom would apply a Vicks or Mentholatum rub to our chests then place a warmed cloth with Vicks over our chests. Sometimes the cloth was wrapped around our necks with the Vicks or Mentholatum and pinned with a safety pin. It did help clear nasal and breathing passages and I thought it felt very soothing.

Larry: When we were growing up most of the men smoked cigarettes, cigars or pipes. Few women smoked. The health hazards of smoking we know today weren't known then. People were aware that smoking caused lung cancer but few seemed to care. When Dad was young he smoked a pipe and the aroma of the pipe smoke smelled pretty good. It seemed natural that I would smoke something too someday.

Larry "smoking" a Pipe

We had a detached garage in the back yard when we lived in the Superintendent's House. One day one of my friends and I discovered a box of cigars in the garage so we decided to light up and share a cigar. It only took a few puffs and we were both deathly ill. I think that is what cured me of ever wanting to smoke anything again.

Household Chores

My Father taught me to work; he did not teach me to love it.
Abraham Lincoln

Barbara: We didn't have a list of chores made up for us. We just knew that all chores in the house were the responsibility of all of us. We made our bed every day and made it well. Mom was a good teacher. Aunt Cleo tells the story of a time when she, Aunt Louise and Mom shared a bed. Aunt Louise and Aunt Cleo made the bed one day and when Mom saw it, she was very annoyed because they had done such a sloppy job of it. Mom told them so and proceeded to make the bed over according to her standard of bed making. Aunt Cleo laughed about the story many years later when she thought of it.

Mom taught me to embroider, crochet, sew (I also took home-economics in high school), and clean thoroughly. Marlene and I would scrub the hardwood floors in the big house on our hands and knees. After scrubbing, we would wax and shine the floors—again on our knees. Grandma Knez told Mom once that she worked us too hard. I don't think so because I remember the great satisfaction I received from seeing the house sparkling clean with everything in its proper place.

> Marlene and I would scrub the hardwood floors in the big house on our hands and knees.

There were no dish-washing machines, so we took turns washing and drying the dishes. Mom and Dad rarely washed dishes although Mom did help out when there were large family gatherings. At such times, I think every pot, pan or dish Mom owned was sitting on the counter waiting to be washed. It was a monumental task.

Mom, Marlene and I did the wash and cleaned house every Saturday. We had double decker tubs for washing the clothes. The wringer on the washing machine would pivot three hundred and sixty degrees allowing us to use two wash tubs and two rinse tubs. I thought it was great fun to run the clothes through the rollers that were part of the wringer. It was a challenge to get the clothes through the rollers without getting your fingers and hand caught. We knew the rules and were extremely careful in getting the job done right.

We learned how to iron. I still remember the time I went over to Mrs. Zinko's house. I was probably not over nine years of age. I could barely reach the ironing board. I dropped the iron and miraculously caught it by the handle before it hit the floor. I was scared to death. Not because I could have had a very serious burn but because Mrs. Zinko might never again let me iron in her house. I could have broken her iron!

I oftentimes ironed my sweater before going to school because of the wrinkles accrued when the sweater was folded (neatly) in the drawer. Mom ironed Dad's shirts and pants. They were cotton and had to have that crisp, sharp look to them for work. I remember her ironing basket. She would sprinkle the clean, dry clothes, roll them up, and put them in the basket until each item had the proper dispersion of water to make it easy to iron and get out the wrinkles. It was a regular weekly task for her but she loved seeing the results of her labor.

One of the jobs that I hated was emptying and washing out the ash trays that were scattered around the house. Dad (and most of the male relatives) was a cigarette smoker and there were always cigarette butts and ashes in the glass trays. I am sure there was a lingering smell of tobacco in the house but, when you grow up in that environment, you become accustomed to the smell.

Larry: As part of our rent, we were required to maintain all the grounds around, not only our house, but also around the bachelor's quarters and the community church. Maybe they weren't as extensive as they seemed to a young boy, but when you had to mow all that grass with a non-motorized push mower it seemed like the size of a farmer's field. And I don't really know how we managed to water it all with only hoses and small sprinklers. Underground irrigations systems were inconceivable!

Christmas time

Ed: Christmas was such a wonderful time. My Mom and Dad didn't have very much money so we would get one present from

Larry, Marlene, Eddie and Barbara - Christmas in the early 1950's

Santa and one present from our parents. I don't know for sure, but I think the kids bought or made modest presents for each other, so we only had three or four presents under the tree at Christmas time. But it was always an enjoyable and special time for us! Because we would go to midnight Mass, sometimes, our parents would let us open presents before Mass. And every once in a while they would let us open our presents after Mass and then stay up and play with the toys and the games until dawn. One year my brother got the Civil War game and Larry and I stayed up and played for hours.

Barbara: Mom made Marlene's and my clothes, even our coats. It was a way to save money and Mom was a great seamstress. She always made the costumes for the school Christmas plays, usually out of crepe paper. Those plays were so much fun. In those days, we didn't have to worry about avoiding the "Christmas" word and everyone wanted to celebrate. The mining company provided each family with a bag with Brach's candy, an apple and an orange. We weren't supposed to get any because Dad didn't belong to the union, but we were given one anyway. Maybe Dad paid for the bags?

Community Activities

Winter in Mt. Harris

Barbara: Winter could be pretty cruel and we felt the sting of snow and ice growing up in the 40's. Once snow fell on the ground in late October, we could expect snow-covered roads until the warmth of spring began to melt the ice. We weren't afraid of contaminated icicles attached to the roofs of the homes and, when we could reach them, enjoyed the cold moisture in our mouths.

As children, we seemed to weather the cold well and Mom made sure we were adequately clothed. Some of the most fun we had was on the old wooden sleds that had metal runners. We had a sledding hill that also served as a path to the school. It was south of highway 40 and extended from the top of the hill to the railroad tracks many yards away. The boys made it so that the sleds would "jump" going down the incline at a very fast speed. I was afraid of the jumps and would try to slow the sled before getting to that point. I particularly remember sledding one night when the moon was full and we could see clearly our path in the snow. It was great. After our activity, we went home and put our feet on an open stove door to thaw out.

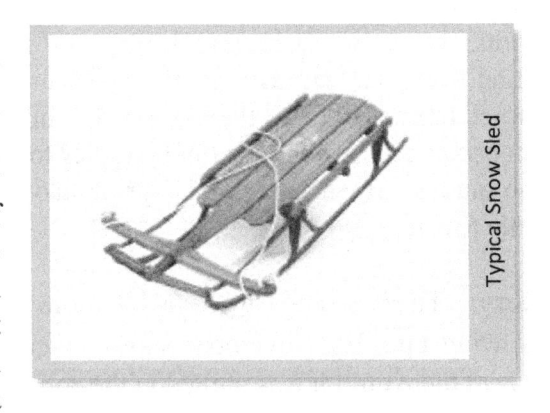

Typical Snow Sled

We also enjoyed being pulled behind the car on our sleds. Dad and our uncles would hitch up the sleds with ropes and attach them like a train to the car. Dad would then drive very slowly on the road in the town. It was a very safe but exceedingly fun activity for us since there was little to no traffic on the Mt. Harris roads. If anyone fell off the sled or turned a sled over, we would yell to Dad to stop. It worked very well.

Although we grew up in ski country, we never learned to ski. Dad did some cross country skiing in his youth but never showed us how to do it. We also learned to ice skate but I don't think we did it very often.

The roads remained snow covered all winter and Mom was very insistent that we wear our rubber boots over our shoes every day to school. On the day Mom said we could forego wearing our boots, we were very happy. It was as if a big weight had been lifted from our feet. By this time of year, the snowy roads had turned to mud since all the roads were unpaved in the town. We "hopscotched" around the mud puddles to avoid getting our feet too muddy. It was a sign that spring had come to our beautiful little town.

Larry: There seemed to be a lot more snow when we were growing up. By November snow covered the ground and it stayed there until it was melted in the spring. Since there was so much snow, we did a lot of playing in it. In Mt. Harris, we had a sledding run from the road coming into the town and it ran down nearly to the railroad tracks. Snowball fights were common and when all the cousins were together we would build large opposing snow forts in the yard and volley snowballs at the opponent's fort, sometime attacking until the forts were destroyed. At times we would tunnel under the snow (it was deep enough to do that) and put candles in the tunnels. It was wonderful to see the snow glowing where the candles were. Out on the Knez ranch, kids on sleds were pulled by a vehicle down the snow packed country roads while others rode on the Antone Knez' snow mobiles.

There was snow pretty much all winter in Mount Harris so the walkways and roads were snowy or sloppy all the while. Almost all shoes were made from leather, both tops to bottoms. This meant that we couldn't get them wet walking through the snow and water because it would ruin them. We wore rubber over-boots or galoshes to protect the shoes. The boys' were black and had buckles all the way up the front. They weren't stylish but they did what they were designed to do.

Galoshes

Another funny thing we did in the winter and other times when it was cold out was wear coats and sweaters and actually button them or zip them up. It seemed like a good idea at the time. Besides, our parents wouldn't have let us out the door if we didn't have a proper coat on when it was cold.

Colorful Personalities

Barbara: Mt. Harris had its share of colorful personalities. As a little girl, I remember "Apple Betty" walking along Highway 40 on her way to Mt. Harris from Bear Valley. She lived alone in a small dwelling at that small community of several people just east of Mt. Harris. The other person who lived there was a fisherman by the name of "Jimmy the Greek." He was connected to our family because he would come into town and stop at the mine office to ask Dad if he would take him (Jimmy) to the Steamboat area to fish. Dad would always say "yes" even though it also entailed going back to Steamboat in about seven days to return Jimmy to his home. Mom was not always thrilled with the idea of two drives to Steamboat but went along with Dad's decision. After Jimmy returned from his fishing adventure, he would cook the fish in deep olive oil that permeated the air around his dwelling.

Luigi "Louie" Valieri was from Italy and carved various figures of animals and other creatures out of driftwood and fallen branches. His yard in Mt. Harris (and later in Craig) was filled with his beautiful and fantastic creations.

Mrs. Kovach lived alone in Mt. Harris and loved to grow vegetables in her garden which she peddled around the town. Mom was always willing to buy something from her even though we had a garden of our own.

Dinah was a very tall, slender, elderly African-American man who would sit on the concrete "fence" that surrounded the non-working fountain and grassy area outside Dad's office. He always dressed in fine clothes and walked with a cane. Dad told me once that Dinah prayed a prayer that was meaningful to Dad and has become a daily prayer of mine. He would say simply, "Lord, take my hand. I want to walk this day with you."

One of the most colorful personalities to come out of Mt. Harris was "Rattlesnake Jack" Carson. Jack was a friend of Dad's and they had great times together. The name "Rattlesnake Jack" came from his practice of rounding up rattlers, putting them in gunny sacks and bringing them to his house to "play" with. He was bitten several times, but the bites didn't seem to affect him that much, according to Dad. Dad said there were times when they would go together to the rim rocks overlooking the town to find the snakes. Dad would sit on very large flat rock with another big rock in his hand to kill the first snake that would attempt a climb onto Dad's rock. Occasionally Jack would hitchhike into town after these adventures. Dad told a story about the time Jack had his gunny sack of snakes when a kind gentleman stopped to pick him up for the ride into Mt. Harris. He asked what was in the sack and when Jack told him, the man immediately slammed on his brakes and told him to get out. It's something any one of us would have done. Jack was also a rather good amateur boxer and would entertain the crowd

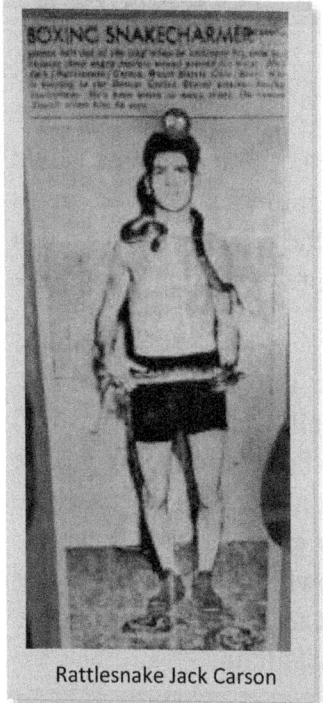

Rattlesnake Jack Carson Playing 3 Part Harmony on trumpets – Three Mouthpieces

Rattlesnake Jack Carson

by wearing a rattler around his neck as he entered the ring. It was a rather novel thing to do.

Ed: My Dad was also a boxer and he trained with Rattlesnake Jack Carson. I believe Carson was the state champion at one time. They regularly used to have boxing fights in Mt. Harris. Sometimes Rattlesnake Jack Carson would be one of the fighters and his signature show was catching rattlesnakes and going into the ring carrying his rattlesnakes. He held a rattlesnake behind the head so it wouldn't bite him and then wrapped it around his neck. When he got to the ring he would take the rattlesnake and throw it out into the crowd. I'm sure that was quite exciting for the spectators.

Dad in Boxing Pose

> His signature show was catching rattlesnakes and going into the ring carrying his rattlesnakes.

Barbara: I don't remember Jack, but I do remember his mother. Each Halloween when we would go Trick or Treating, she would make her house the scariest in town. We would get as far as the front gate and then debate whether or not we had the courage to enter the yard since we knew she was going to pop out of nowhere and give us a big scare. In the end, we always decided to go toward her house anyway but it wasn't because we weren't afraid.

Mom, Dad, Barbara, Marlene and Larry

Mom, Barbara and Marlene

103

Rutherford Music

Barbara: The Rutherford/Squire genes contained within them a wealth of music. Music was a part of the Rutherford family life from the time Grandma Squire married Grandpa Rutherford. The Squire family was seeped in music and Grandma, a pianist/violinist, taught Grandpa how to fiddle. Uncle Leonard told us that the family would gather at a Squire home and after dinner, someone would say, "Let's make music," and the instruments would appear out of everywhere. The family would play deep into the night.

From what I can gather, Grandma Daisy and her sister Pearl were vocalists and loved to sing together. When Pearl died at a rather young age, Daisy never really recovered her zest for music. Although she was the pianist of the dance band that came out of the family, I never once saw her play the piano. Once she set it aside (because of Pearl's death?), she never touched it again.

That was not the case with the Rutherford children. I became very acquainted with those siblings in the world of music. It was said of Uncle Leonard that he couldn't approach any instrument without picking it up and, within minutes, play it. Grandpa bought him a saxophone and told him not to touch it until he could have lessons. That afternoon, when Grandpa was walking home from work, he could hear the sound of a saxophone several houses

Uncle Francis on the Guitar and Dad on the Mandolin

away. He knew who had picked up the instrument. The temptation to do so was too great for Uncle Leonard.

Grandma played the piano; Grandpa fiddled; Dad played the mandolin (or banjo or piano or drums or accordion); Uncle Francis the guitar; Uncle Leonard the sax or piano; Uncle Loren the trumpet and Aunt Wanda sang. It was a wonderful band and the family group was called into service throughout the years they were growing up. During the Depression it provided needed funds for the family. I was acquainted with the band as a small child because Dad would still play for dances and practice sessions were held at Grandma and Grandpa's house. This was after Grandma and Grandpa stopped playing. Aunt Carol, the wife of Uncle Leonard, was a phenomenal pianist and could play ANYTHING by ear. She also could play any piece in any key asked of her. It was simply amazing. She would be part of those jam sessions. It was here that I heard all the jazz music of the 40's.

Mom's family was not musical but she was the one who insisted that we take piano lessons. Mom and Dad bought an upright piano that had a wonderful tone and was part of their living room furniture until the day Dad died. I still remember how happy I was when that piano became part of our furniture in the cinder block house. As soon as I could read, Mom found a teacher in Steamboat (Mrs. Lea Gilbert) who would instruct Marlene and me for about four years. She was a very good teacher and I made wonderful progress--mainly because Mom followed her command that we practice a half hour ever day as a beginner. Before I moved on to Mrs. Price, I was practicing an hour a day. The clock was sitting on the piano and, after school, we couldn't move until all practice time was behind us. I think Marlene took the time rather well, but I wanted to play

> Mom and Dad bought an upright piano that had a wonderful tone and was part of their living room furniture until the day Dad died.

outside. I remember the times I was sitting at the piano with tears wetting the surface of the keys because I couldn't do what I wanted to do. The cost of our beginning half-hour lesson was fifty cents. When we advanced to a forty-five minute lesson, the cost went up to seventy-five cents. Mom drove us to Steamboat every Saturday morning the entire time we took lessons with Mrs. Gilbert. It was truly a commitment on her part.

When Mrs. Price said that she could teach us, Mom stopped the trips to Steamboat. Mrs. Price knew her music but wasn't as demanding as Mrs. Gilbert. She gave instructions that would allow more flexibility in practice time so I didn't make as much progress with her. Nevertheless, I did love to play the piano and thought sight-reading was great. I took lessons until I reached eighth grade and then Mom allowed me to stop. Maybe Mrs. Price decided not to teach anymore. Or maybe she moved away. I don't remember but I had enough background in piano to serve as accompanist for the high school choir for a time and loved doing it. Mom would encourage us to just sit down and play the piano which we did quite often.

When I went to Loretto Heights, Sister Katherine Therese noticed that I had some background in music and asked me to come to her music studio and play for her. I chose *Malagueña* for my piece and she liked it well enough to offer me a piano performance scholarship my freshman year. She didn't know it at the time (and neither did I) but that scholarship set me on a course toward a major in music which I got at Webster College in St. Louis.

Larry: As long as I can remember Dad had a dance band that played in several venues around Northwestern Colorado. Although the composition of the band changed from time to time over the years, Dad played the piano, Uncle Loren played the trumpet and Junior Rolando played the saxophone. Drummers seemed to come and go and my brother Ed played the trombone in the later years. It brought in a little extra money to the family but, regardless, Dad really loved it. He named the band the *Rhythmaires*.

Ed: My father grew up in the Mt. Harris area and told me about the Rutherford family dance band. My grandma played the piano, my grandpa played the violin, my Uncle Leonard played the saxophone, Uncle Loren played the trumpet, my Dad played the mandolin, Uncle Francis played the guitar, Aunt Wanda played the piano and sang. They traveled all over the area playing for dances and had a great time

Later, Dad had his own dance band and when I was old enough, possibly a junior in high school, he asked me if I wanted to be in his dance band. I said, "sure." I would be able to make a little money and have a good time doing it. Junior Rolando was in the band and played the saxophone and clarinet. Dad played the piano. A guy from Steamboat played the bass and then another fellow played the drums. I can't remember their names. Uncle Loren would play the trumpet. It was a great part-time job for me.

Dad told me about a time when he went out with Junior Rolando and some other guys. Once, Dad was just driving down the street and Junior rolled out of the car. When he went around the corner the door had come open. No problem. Dad just went around the block and picked Junior up and they just continued on their way.

Hunting and Fishing - Mt. Harris

Fish Creek Falls near Steamboat Springs

Barbara: Dad loved to fish in the summer but fishing never took precedence over attending Sunday Mass. As little children, we loved going to an early morning Mass and then trekking off to some remote fishing area where we would enjoy a campfire with all the food cooked in cast iron cookware. Fresh caught fish was part of the noonday/evening picnic fare. If we didn't go fishing, we would often just drive to Fish Creek Falls where we enjoyed immensely the beauty of the woods and the roar of the falls. We were allowed to play on the rocks at the base of the falls as long as we didn't get too close to the edge of the rushing water. I loved being there!

When we went fishing, we would gather with other family members and drive to the mountains. We packed boxes of food to be cooked over a campfire and ate some of the fish which the guys would catch in the mountain streams. We were sometimes allowed to fish, too, which meant Dad spent as much time baiting our hooks as he did fishing. He never complained, however, and we loved it.

Hunting for deer and elk was part of both families' lives. We grew up eating wild meat and liked it very much. Sometimes, members of the family would poach the meat and we were sworn to secrecy about the presence of a deer or elk that might have been hanging in the garage on the ranch.

Ed: Rabbit Ears Pass was one of our favorite places to go fishing. We would go up there but at times we were just miserable. On one hand, it was fun because we caught fish in these tiny streams. We would have to sneak up the bank and drop our hook into the water and, sure enough, we would have a fish on our line almost right away. The problem was there were a million mosquitoes around these streams. They were so thick you would slap your arm and kill ten. Unfortunately, there wasn't very good repellant at the time so you just had to try to ignore them the best you could.

Eddie, Larry and Ann Rutherford in the Mountains

The Knez Ranch

Barbara: If we attended Mass in Craig (Father Slattery was the parish priest when I was a small child), we would join all the Knez clan at this sacred celebration and then drive out to one of the family farms for the rest of the day. We loved to be at Grandma and Grandpa Knez's home because there was so much to do while there

Knez Homestead (Abandoned)

and Grandma introduced us to so many interesting and fun things on the ranch. These included getting the newly laid eggs from the chicken house, running the milk separator, helping to make cottage cheese, watching her slaughter a chicken or two for dinner, picking chokecherries, or harvesting the goodies from her garden grown on the hillside next to the road. Two things Grandma said to us while we were there--if we were playing on her piano, "If you are playing that for me, you can stop" and, "I love to see you come and I love to see you go."

Grandma was a very colorful person. I have fond memories of her taking us to town where she would pick up ice (from Mr. Hansen) for her ice box and sell eggs to friends and acquaintances in town. One name I remember was that of a little lady named Mrs. Hartman who lived in a small duplex on the north side of Highway 40 as you entered town (across from the

OP restaurant today). Stories abounded in the family about Grandma's bootlegging experiences during Prohibition. She made her own whiskey and peddled it in town. Grandpa was fearful that she would get caught so he ended her operation by hiding the "distillery" in the fields where she couldn't find it. I also watched her make Dandelion Wine and her own root beer. Her special treat for us was making popcorn balls. Yes, it was fun being around her when we were little children!

I also picture Grandma Knez getting ready for Mass. She would be running later than Grandpa where he (and Marlene and I) would be sitting in the car outside honking the horn. She would emerge from the house rushing out the front door of the porch trying to get the large hat pin into her hat and through the bun in her hair. What a great memory. She also taught me how to crochet. There were two chairs situated on either side of the radio -- one for Grandpa and one for her where she would sit and crochet. On the floor between the chairs was a dish of candy with lemon drops for Grandma and candy corn for Grandpa (or was it the other way around?).

When I was a teenager, she bought me a diamond ring with a small chip diamond from Sather's jewelry. She also bought me my favorite of all-times green coat when I was a junior in high school. I loved that coat and was devastated when, while visiting Uncle Loren and Aunt Doris, I leaned up against their coal fired stove and scorched my beautiful coat. I tried everything I could to repair it, but the damage was done.

Uncle Antone and Aunt Cleo always invited us to their home, too, where we had the run of the hills. Rattlesnakes were always a source of fear for me so I didn't want to wander too far into the terrain around the house but found plenty of activity without doing so. Sometimes, Tom and Ralph would saddle up the horse and we were allowed to go horseback riding. Other times, we would venture over the fence into the cattle corral where Marlene, along with her male cousins, would try to ride the calves. I had an interior fear of any activity that I deemed dangerous to my life.

All my relatives on both sides of the family ate wild meat daily. Deer and elk were at the heart of our main meals and we loved it. Everyone had freezers by the time I was about five/six years old and as soon as the meat became depleted, the guys would be out in the fields and hills getting more, in season or out. Often times, deer or elk was hanging in the garage to age a bit and we were under strict orders never to mention that fact to anyone since it could mean hefty fines if detected by a game warden out of season.

> Often times, a deer or elk was hanging in the garage to age a bit and we were under strict orders to never mention that fact.

Hunting was a loved sport in the family but killing an animal was never "just for fun." It was always because the meat supply was low and someone in the family needed to replenish the supply. Our main meal was quite standard and varied little day to day. We had mashed potatoes and milk gravy, canned vegetable, deer, elk or chicken. We ate lettuce during the summer when we could get it out of the garden but rarely had it during the winter. Desserts were exquisitely made by the women in the family but were not an everyday treat. These desserts came out when the families were gathered together.

Ed: Everything around Mt. Harris was focused on the outdoors. We were outside all the time. We never really camped that much, but we were always in the mountains. I remember going up to Hahn's Peak and the Seed House to fish. Both were near Steamboat Springs. We would also go to Trapper's Lake which at that time was one of the first places that was infested by pine beetles. All the trees were dead but it was still a beautiful lake. It is about 50 miles west of Meeker, Colorado, and is the second largest natural lake in Colorado.

Larry: The dirt road to Trapper's Lake is long and winding. It always made me car sick and we had to stop a couple of times along the way so I could get out. One time when we went up there it had rained and the road was muddy and slick. At one point the car started sliding off the road toward a very long and steep slope. Dad did his best to get us back on the road but at least one wheel was over the edge. We were all inside and were afraid to get out and destabilize the car any more. We were scared to death but Mom was hysterical, not without reason of course, particularly after being in that accident with Grandpa. I believe relatives were with us and they managed to push, pull and/or tow us back to safety without further incident, but that was a close call.

Delores Knez, Eddie and Larry

Larry: In the '40s and '50s around Mt. Harris and Craig there was no light pollution. If you were in the country and the moon was not out it was pitch dark beyond the scope of the farm light. The stars were brilliant and made a sparkling blanket across the night sky. When we were at Aunt Cleo and Uncle Antone's ranch out in that darkness you could hear the coyotes howling and sometimes we heard the scream of mountain lions. That was ominous and chilling. When I was very young I remember being out at the Squire's ranch visiting one night and they had no electricity. The farm house was only lighted with lanterns. The rooms, beyond the light of the lamps, were totally dark and a bit spooky. It was pitch dark in the house and it was even darker outside surrounding their home. That takes a bit of getting used to.

Milner and Steamboat Springs

The Milner Gas Station

Ed: My grandmother (Daisy) and grandfather (Coke) on my Dad's side retired in Milner and my grandfather bought a little gas station where he sold gas and little knick-knacks and snacks. His best friend was a kind old black man named Joe Brown. He used to come over and talk to my grandfather and he would talk with us, too. He had a wife but I never did see him with her. He would go to the Mickeletti Mercan- tile grocery store across the street. It was just an old time grocery store.

Grandpa and Grandma Rutherford

Grandpa and Grandma Rutherford

We would go up to Milner to visit when we lived in Mt. Harris but particularly when we lived in Craig. It seemed that we would take the trip just about every weekend to see my Grandma and

Grandpa. It was about 40 minutes away which felt like a long way for a kid. Did we have to go? I think I said that once, and Dad told me never say that to him again.

Grandpa sold five-cent candy bars and I would get a *Baby Ruth*. My sister loved *Cherry Mashes* so every time she was around she would have a *Cherry Mash*. Then the price went up to 10 cents and then 15 cents. Initially, the candy bars were small but then they started getting larger along with the price.

Driving to Steamboat Springs

Ed: I remember going to Mass every Sunday. We would drive to Steamboat to go to Mass and then in the summer after Mass we would take Father Prinster up to Fish Creek Falls for a picnic. It was a rustic place at that time. One time we were returning from Steamboat, probably on a Sunday, we were driving along this long stretch of sand rocks east of town and the police had traffic stopped because a car had gone off the cliff. It landed on its top on the railroad tracks below. I remember Mom being very distressed. I didn't exactly understand what was going on and she didn't really want to tell me. She just said something terrible happened and we should pray for the people, which we did.

Aunt Dorris and Uncle Loren Rutherford

We would stop along the way at Mrs. Kovache's house to buy some eggs. We would also pull over at a little spring (Elk River Spring) that was just before you got to the sand rocks and Mom would fill up some jugs of water.

Speaking of water, I remember being in the bathtub in Mt. Harris when we had a big surprise. The town processed its own water and it had the community water tank on top of a hill near the mine. I was in the bathtub when all of a sudden parts of frogs were coming out of the spout. Oh my gosh! Mom was pretty upset. She shouted to me, "Get out of the tub! Get out of the tub!"

Aunt Juanita (Rutherford) and Uncle Alfred Camiletti at the Elk River Spring

Steamboat Springs Swimming Pool

Ed: Sometimes when we went to Steamboat Springs, we would go swimming in the pool. It was such a beautiful pool but the very large outside pool was a bit chilly. It was still fine to swim in but the natural spring pools inside were really hot and comfortable. I don't know if I remember this story or if someone told me, as I was only three years old at the time. My Mom and Dad were talking to Fr. Prinster alongside the pool and they weren't watching me. I fell into the pool or jumped into the water and halfway through the conversation Fr. Prinster said, "Well, I think that's Eddie on the bottom of the pool." He became pretty excited and bounded right in, clerics and all, and brought me up from the bottom of the pool.

Larry: We also went swimming at Juniper Hot Springs 30 miles west of Craig out in the middle of nowhere. It was near the Yampa River and, to my recollection, it was open to everyone at no cost. There was a rustic building to change in but not much more. The swimming pool was situated outdoors over natural hot springs and, although there was concrete surrounding the pool, the bottom was just sand. The water percolated up from

Uncle Antone, Uncle Raymond, Uncle Joseph and Grandpa

No Rattlesnakes Allowed

the bottom and was quite warm and comfortable. It was a great place to have a picnic and a dip in the pool. And we only found a rattlesnake on the front step once. It was dispatched quickly. No rattlesnakes were allowed.

Relatives

Grandparents

Barbara: This is how I remember Dad's parents. My Dad's father, Grandpa Coke liked to tease us children and kept asking me when I was going to learn how to play "Turkey in the Straw." When I finally did learn it, I couldn't wait to play it for him. He, also, was the one who pulled out my first baby tooth because it was very loose and I didn't want to wait until Dad got home from work to have it done. Grandma was always

Dad, Grandma Rutherford, Aunt Doris (Monteith) Rutherford, Francis Rutherford Leonard Rutherford and Ralph Henderson

very quiet and pleasant in manner. Whenever we visited we just sat in a chair and didn't move.

We lived out the maxim that "children should be seen and not heard" at her house. With that in mind, it baffled me how she could have raised seven children. Her house was totally spotless. She demonstrated the adage that "cleanliness was next to godliness". The story was told that she had next to nothing in material goods but always had a bar of soap to make sure the children's clothes were clean and pressed. She also was stoic in how she bore pain, especially child-birth pain. From what Dad said, his parents were very strict with the few rules they had. The children could run freely around the town but always had to be home for dinner—not a minute late.

Mom's parents were Catholic and loved children. We had the run of the farm whenever we visited them. On our way up to the farmhouse, we would sometimes stop at the entrance of the mine to see if Grandpa was working there that day. On occasion, Grandma would take us children with her into town. I remember how she used to pick up blocks of ice for her ice box from Mr. Hansen and how she would stop and visit an older woman by the name of Mrs. Hartman. Grandma would make a tasty chicken and noodles dinner. She let us help with the milk separator and would make popcorn balls for us. We got to gather the eggs from the chicken house and help pick vegetables in the garden. We watched her many times as she butchered chickens to eat. We had to share the gizzard because all the grandchildren loved it.

Grandma raised her children, broke the land for the farm, cooked for the miners, and sometimes worked in the mine. Being on that farm was so much fun. Grandpa was much more serious but he loved his grandchildren. He would hold us on his lap and give us hugs. He was always German prompt and when it was time to leave for Mass on Sunday, he would get the car, stop in front of the house and honk the horn. Grandma, who was more relaxed, would come running with her hat pin in one hand and hat in the other. When Grandpa became ill, he would eat lots of garlic thinking it would heal him. He had one surgery for his cancer and he thought he would get well but his good times didn't last long. He was brought home from the hospital where Aunt Louise helped to nurse him in his final days.

Grandma Knez

Ed: My grandmother lived with us until she had to go to a nursing home. It was such a disheartening thing to see her decline as she got old. She was such an upstanding strong woman but by the time she had to go to the nursing home she couldn't control her bodily functions. It was very difficult for my mother. And then, in her dementia, she would accuse Mom of stealing from her. My Mom didn't take it personally because she understood and loved my grandmother so much.

I remember my Mom telling me a story about my Dad and my Mom getting in financial difficulties. They went to my grandmother because she did have some money and so they asked her to help them out. I think she loaned them some but I don't think she gave them that much. It was some help, but the last thing she said before they left the little meeting was, "I will do it this time but never, ever ask again."

Ed: My Mom and Dad asked my Grandma Rutherford to babysit for my sisters one time when they were really in a bind. It was kind of an emergency situation and my grandmother's response was, "No, I won't. I raised mine, you raise yours." My Grandma Rutherford was very stern and a little bit grim. Dad's Aunt Margie, who had severe edema in her legs and had difficulty walking. She lived in Steamboat Springs and I remember going to visit her there. She was always very kind and nice and I thought she was just wonderful.

Dad, Larry, Eddie and Aunt Margie

Aunts, Uncles and Cousins

Uncle Rube Squire was Grandma's brother. I would always love it when he would come to the house and would tell stories about rodeos and what happened out in the "wild west." He lived in the area around Steamboat Springs where he was born. One of the stories concerned the sheep men and the cattlemen in Routt

THE SQUIRES—Back Row: Shirley, Daisy (Grandma), Edith, Annie, May, Margie
Front Row: Andy, Coke (Grandpa), Rube, Frank, Mike

County where a conflict over fences almost came to a shootout. The cattlemen wanted the properties fenced but the sheep men didn't because they thought they needed the sheep to roam the countryside. The cattlemen didn't like that because when the sheep would graze they would bite down and pull up the grass roots and all. They would leave the ground bare. The cattlemen, consequently, would fence the land. One morning when the cattlemen were busy putting up fence, the sheep men rode up packing their six guns on their sides. An intense argument ensued and it was a very nervous standoff. The sheep men planned on taking the fences down and the cattlemen swore that the fences would stay up. They were eye to eye and it came down to who would draw his gun first.

> **They were eye to eye and it came down to who would draw their gun first.**

Uncle Alfred and Aunt Neat Camiletti lived on a beautiful place just outside Milner up a draw. Once when we were there Pat Camiletti fell into their water cistern. Someone, luckily, was outside and heard her crying out for help. Everyone rushed over and pulled her out of the water. It was particularly frightening because she was very young and could have easily drowned there.

Aunt Marie and Uncle Bo Turner lived just outside of Mt. Harris in a modest little house on the way to Hayden just past the rim rocks and across the bridge on the Yampa.

Aunt Carol, Uncle Bo, Aunt Neat and Aunt Marie

Barbara: My own recollection of Aunt Wanda's death is rather sketchy. She died in June of 1955 and the Sisters of Loretto were staying with us while teaching a week of religious education for the children. Since the sisters were there, we stayed home with them while Mom and Dad drove to Grand Junction for the funeral. I was fourteen years of age – old enough to watch Eddie during the day. I was not too perceptive and was, I guess, too young to see the sorrowful ramifications of her early death. I don't know who cared for us prior to her death, when Mom and dad went to see her in the hospital. I just know that they were able to be with her for a bit of time while she was hospitalized.

Aunt Wanda and Uncle Fred moved from Mt. Harris to Clifton, Colorado, when Ron (their oldest child) was probably about 6 years old. It was a three hour drive from Mt. Harris so we saw the family rarely after that. When Aunt Wanda was in her 30's, she was expecting her 5th baby and the family came to Mt. Harris. This is Uncle Leonard's account of the visit as told to me (Barbara) on Sunday, January 28, 2007. I wrote down the memories he related to me since he was an eyewitness to all that was happening in our families at the time.

"Aunt Wanda and Uncle Fred visited Aunt Neat during Wanda's fifth pregnancy. The Rutherford family gathered together to see Wanda and Fred who had come to Milner from Grand Junction. When Grandma Daisy saw Wanda, she knew there was something seriously wrong because Wanda appeared to be very ill. It turned out she had a serious kidney disease. The family sensed she didn't have long to live.

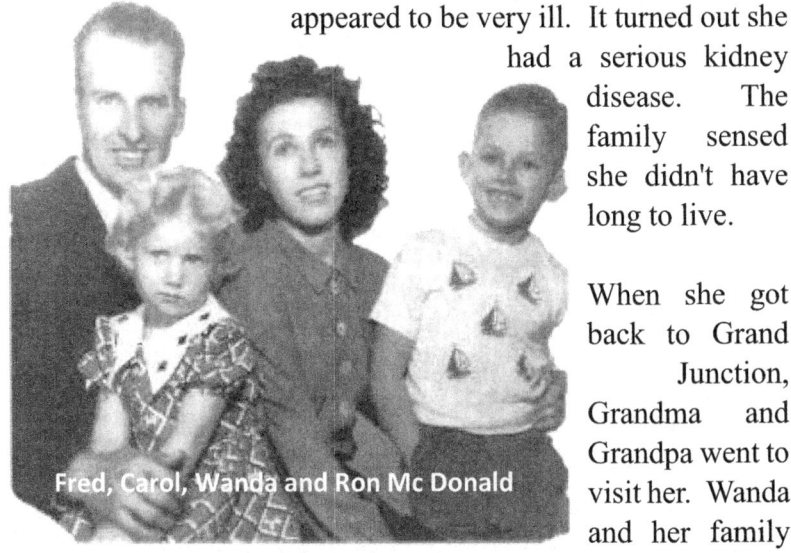

When she got back to Grand Junction, Grandma and Grandpa went to visit her. Wanda and her family were living in extreme poverty and there was next to no food in the house. Grandpa went out and bought over a hundred dollars' worth of food, which was a lot of money in 1955. Fred had a heart condition in which he would pass out without warning. He was unable to keep a job but did seasonal work in his Dad's fruit orchards in Palisade.

Fred, Carol, Wanda and Ron Mc Donald

Wanda had the baby and, although she was very ill, she insisted on going home with her new baby. Most of the Rutherford family had traveled to Grand Junction to be with her. Uncle Francis and Aunt Doris stayed with Wanda and Fred. They heard her moaning one night and they took her to the hospital. By that time, she was in a coma and didn't regain consciousness."

> Wanda and her family were living in extreme poverty and there was next to no food in the house

Ed: In recalling my Knez family, it seems we were always with them. Mostly we were at Uncle Antone and Aunt Cleo's house. Uncle Antone was just a fun guy and it was always enjoyable going to visit his place. Bobby Knez was a good friend of mine

Joseph, Raymond, Antone, Grandma, Grandpa, Mom and Louise

as well as his brother, Delbert. We liked to ride horses or we would grab our .22 rifles and set out walking up the road to my Grandma's house that was on a road that ran back on the property. We would shoot at pretty much anything we saw. We also rode horses at my Uncle Charlie and Aunt Louise Fedinic's ranch. They would frequently saddle them up and off we would go into the hills.

Larry: Some of our cousins did very funny things. I was not there to observe these shenanigans but when I was young I heard them told and retold.

Cars in Craig weren't generally locked up when parked. Convenient automatic locks were virtually unknown then. One cousin acquired a gorilla costume and got into the back seat of a friend's car and hid down between the seats. As his friend drove off and started down the road he quietly got up, tapped the driver on the shoulder, looked into the rear view mirror and growled. The friend nearly had a heart attack and almost ran off the road.

Another time a cousin had gone into town on his horse to tip a few at the White Horse Inn tavern in downtown Craig. Maybe he stayed longer than he should have but when left he mounted his horse backwards. Apparently, the horse knew the way home, although it was several miles. He proceeded precariously out of town and down the county road. The sheriff noticed the spectacle as he passed and turned on his lights and pulled up behind the horse and rider. He got out of the car and approached the rider. Before he could say anything the inebriated cowboy said, "What's wrong offither, wuth I speeding?"

Uncle Antone was always a lot of fun and liked a good laugh. There were a lot of comical things he did and this was one of them. Mom and Dad had a picnic in the backyard of their house and invited all of her family over. Everyone was visiting and having a great time when Uncle Antone had picked up a beer and was striding across the yard to see something he thought was interesting. At the same time, he was talking and looking back toward the family instead of forward. He ran his head right into the crossbar of the clothes line. It knocked him down to the ground and flat on his back. Before getting up he said with a big smile: "I didn't spill a drop" referring to his beer that he was carrying. He was correct. None of us saw a single drop of beer come out of the beer bottle when he slammed to the ground. Everyone had a good laugh.

The Car Accident on Wise Hill and Marie Carter

Barbara: In 1927, Grandpa Knez was driving the Carter family home to Morapos (beyond Hamilton) when the car slid off the road at the bottom of Wise Hill, south of Craig. Grandpa was always afraid of meeting cars on curves so had driven too close to the edge as a precaution. It was tragic because Roselin Edwards Carter, Grandma's daughter from her first marriage, was killed along with Roselin's eleven-month-old baby boy. Mom, Uncle Antone, Uncle Joseph, Marie Carter and Roselin's husband Richard Carter were also in the car.

When the car went off the road, it rolled over. Mom had a broken collar bone and Uncle Joseph had a broken leg. Grandpa was knocked unconscious and was in a coma for several weeks and was unable to go to Roselin's funeral. Immediately after the accident, Mom said that she and Uncle Antone walked up the incline toward the road and sat down. While sitting there, Mom was quite sure that she heard a baby cry for a few minutes. No one really believed her, according to Mom, but she swore it was true.

Grandma Knez grieved for Roselin until the end of her life and would weep if anyone began to talk about her. Grandma told me that Grandpa Knez never once

Roelin Carter

mentioned Roselin's name after the accident. It was probably his own way of grieving.

The Carter family was very, very poor and when "Little Marie" Carter was a young teen, she came to live with Grandma and Grandpa's family. She was just a bit younger than Mom. Mom told me that when Little Marie arrived, she had next to no extra clothing and had no shoes. Mom and Aunt Louise wanted to give her everything they had because they were so sad at seeing her poverty. The three young girls shared a double bed. I don't know how long Marie lived at the Knez ranch but I think she became one of the family and close to Mom while she was there.

> Mom and Aunt Louise wanted to give her everything they had because they were so sad at seeing her poverty.

Aunt Grace and Uncle Joseph

Mom and Aunt Grace

Barbara: Aunt Grace was married to Uncle Raymond. She was an interesting woman, from my perspective. She loved to search for Indian arrowheads on the family property and would bring out her "treasures" whenever we asked her to do so. There were high rocks next to her home and we loved to climb on them whenever we visited this Knez family. We were told that there were no rattlesnakes on that side of the ridge across from Uncle Antone's property which gave us peace of mind when exploring the rocks.

Aunt Grace got breast cancer when she was (I think) in her late thirties. In those days, cancer of any kind was a killer. She had surgery and was told if she survived five years, the cancer would be gone. She made it about four years, and one day while we were visiting the family, she took Mom into a bedroom and told her the cancer had returned. Ramona was the oldest of the five children and was about fifteen years of age at the time (as far as I remember).

When Aunt Grace was hospitalized as the cancer progressed, Ramona wanted to visit her mother and was told "no" because the hospital had strict rules about children under eighteen visiting patients. Ramona resented that because she wanted to say goodbye to her mother.

Mom and Aunt Grace

The day before Aunt Grace died, she told everyone who visited her that "The Lord cometh to get me." Uncle Raymond told us that he didn't expect her to die that night. It appeared to all who visited her that she was still too alert and strong to be expecting to die but she did die that night.

> I still remember Grandma Knez weeping silently for her dying son.

Uncle Joseph also died young - in his forties - but his death was a farming accident in 1959. We had just moved into the house on Tucker Street and I hadn't yet left for Kentucky. When we got word that he was being brought to the hospital after catching his arm in the combine while trying to fix it, we all gathered in our living room and waited for the ambulance to arrive since we lived directly across from the hospital. I still remember Grandma Knez weeping silently for her dying son.

What struck me about the account of his death was that he asked to have a priest sent to the site of the accident along with machinists who could cut his arm loose from the combine. He was always a very faithful, devout Catholic. He was still alive when he was brought to the hospital but because of the loss of blood, he didn't survive. We were told that Uncle Antone and Uncle Raymond gave blood to save him but the doctor said the donated blood couldn't make it through his system fast enough to keep him alive.

Joseph and Virginia Knez and Louise and Charlie Fedinic

Uncle Joseph was the father of nine children. The youngest was a mere two years old. I wasn't mature enough to think about Aunt Virginia and what must have been going through her mind as she faced single motherhood at that Moment in her life.

Ed: We were with the Knez family all the time. Joseph was the oldest and I still remember that in 1959, we had just gotten our house built and Grandma was at the house so I think she was already living in the back apartment when we saw the ambulances come flying in. We were looking out the window of our dining room because we lived right across the street from the hospital. A car came up after the ambulance. It was my Aunt Virginia. When she got out of the car my Grandma just about fainted because she knew what was happening wasn't good. Grandma and Dad walked across the street and confirmed it was Uncle Joseph that they were bringing in. He had gotten his arm caught one of the pulleys on the combine out in the field and couldn't get out. He tried to cut his arm off but he passed out and he bled to death out in the field. It was a terrible time for the family.

Louise (Knez) Fedinic, Helen Knez and Cleo Knez

Ed: One time we were coming home from Denver with my Uncle Charlie (Fedinic. He was driving the car and; as he entered the Eisenhower tunnel, he took his hands off the steering wheel and shouted, "I can't see! I can't see!" My Aunt Louise (Fedinic), my Mom and I were in the back seat. My Dad wasn't there. So the car was going down the road without anyone holding onto

> As he got into the tunnel he raised his hands off the steering wheel and shouted, "I can't see! I can't see."

the steering wheel. My aunt jumped over the seat and grabbed the steering wheel. We didn't know what was wrong with him, but he just started saying, "I can't see! I can't see!"

Uncle Antone, Dad, Larry and Uncle Raymond

Barbara: Marlene and Ralph were building their house in Craig and, as with other family members, they borrowed money from Uncle Raymond. It was totally a business agreement, which Ralph liked, so they were contracted to repay a certain amount on a certain day. At one of the payment days, they gave Uncle Raymond a check. He looked at it and told them to write another. It was either one penny short or one penny too much.

When Uncle Raymond was in his seventies, he was stopped at a stop sign when an old timer in Craig who had known him a long time pulled up behind him. Uncle Raymond wouldn't move, so the man was furious and approached Uncle Raymond's car on foot. They were having a very heated argument when

Exactly what was your problem?

133

Uncle Raymond reached down under his seat and pulled out a gun. At that point, the argument ended.

When Mom and Dad had Uncle Raymond build the house on Tucker Street, they added an apartment onto the main house for Grandma Knez to live in. Dad, Grandma and Uncle Raymond had agreed upon the dimensions of the apartment but when Uncle Raymond finished the add-on, the living room and kitchen area had been reduced by several feet. Dad was furious and Grandma Knez wept when she saw how little space she was to reside in.

One time Uncle Raymond was driving on the Interstate in Arizona when a police officer drove behind him and turned on his lights. Uncle Raymond stopped his car right there in the middle of the Interstate. When the officer approached and reprimanded him and told him to get to the side of the road immediately, Uncle Raymond told him that he always stops right away when the police turn on their lights behind him. Uncle Raymond's offense: driving too slowly on an Interstate.

When Mom was a small child, Grandpa Knez would occasionally bring candy home for the children when he went into town. Everyone would quickly dispense with the candy, everyone except Uncle Raymond. He would mooch candy from his siblings and once the candy was gone, he would bring out his portion and eat it in front of them. Mom couldn't believe he would do that.

Uncle Raymond appeared to be stingy with his money but was generous to those he thought were genuinely in need. Dad was aware of his generosity because Dad was the accountant for the St. Michael's Credit Union and saw the money that Uncle Raymond used to help the poor.

When I attended Loretto Heights College, he came to visit me. I was surprised to see him. As he was leaving, he quickly handed me a twenty dollar bill and left. That was like a fortune to me because I had very little spending money at my disposal.

Larry: Uncle Raymond had a funny sense of humor. We were told a story about a time when a man bought property adjacent

Grandma Knez, Uncle Joseph, Mom, Dad, and Uncle Antone

to his and commenced building a house on it. He graded an access road to the construction site from the county road. Uncle Raymond would visit the man regularly as the building proceeded. One day the man told Uncle Raymond that construction was nearly complete and they would be moving in soon. Uncle Raymond replied, "So how are you going to get to your house?" "What are you talking about?" his neighbor asked. "Well, your only access to your house is across my property and I am not going to give you the right of way." They argued and argued and finally the man ran to his pickup and took out his rifle and started shooting. He didn't hit Uncle Raymond but I think they came to some mutually satisfactory agreement.

> Finally, the man ran to his pickup and took out his rifle and started shooting.

The BB Gun and Tommy Joe

Barbara: If I recall Tom's eye injury correctly, Ralph was shooting a BB gun. No one was in sight but, as he fired a shot, Tom came around the corner of the bunkhouse at Grandma Knez's and the BB pellet hit Tom squarely in the pupil of his eye. Tom lost use of his eye that day and had his eye replaced with a glass eye. Uncle Antone was distressed beyond description but knew it was just an accident. I think he threw the BB guns out and said no one in his family would ever use another one again.

Mine Closing

End of an Era

Barbara: The final years of the mine were sad ones. A sign would be posted in Dad's office each day stating whether or not the mine would be operating the following day. I remember seeing the men milling around waiting for word. There was much poverty. Dad didn't remember Mt. Harris with fond memories because of the poverty. He called it a dirty, little, coal mining camp.

Ed: There came the time for the mine to close at Mt. Harris. I believe it was 1958. Dad had to decide what we were going to do next and that's when he gave the dogs away and we moved to Craig. We didn't have a home in Craig so we stayed with our Grandma Knez who was living in a house across from the park. It worked out fine. At the same time, she had two ladies, Miss Hortense and another old lady that she took care of at her house.

Uncle Raymond was a carpenter and builder so my Dad hired him to build our house. We needed lumber to build it so Dad bought two little houses in Mt. Harris. We frequently had to go back and forth to Mt. Harris to salvage the lumber.

Barbara: I lived in Mt. Harris from my birth in 1940 until I was nearly 18 years old. Maybe Dad was right in saying it was just a dirty, little, coal mining town where there was always poverty before us but, for me, it was a happy time. It was all that Dad said it was but it was also a town connected to a very simple way of life where it seemed that people really cared about each other. I will always remember my childhood growing up there and never forget the good people who crossed my path. God prepares us for things to come by presenting events in our past that make us grow. I think that my experiences of growing up in Mt. Harris were the source of many blessings and I am thankful to a good God who made it so through my wonderful parents and my siblings Marlene, Larry and Edward. May God continue to bless us all.

RUTHERFORD
2018

Part Two

THE BIG CITY

Craig

The population of Craig between 1960 and 1970 was about 4000. It had an interesting history. Between the mid-sixteenth century to the end of the 19th century Moffat County was occupied by a group of Ute Indians called the Yampa or "root eaters." In 1868 a treaty with the Utes granted them nearly all of the Western third of Colorado, the northern boundary being just south of present day Moffat County. The arrival of settlers drawn by mining and the railroad crossing the Rocky Mountains

Craig, Colorado, Victory Way Facing West, 1960's

to the east put pressure on the Ute winter campsites. After the government failed to provide promised provisions and supplies the Indians reached a breaking point. In 1879 the Indians rebelled against Indian Agent Nathan C. Meeker in the town of Meeker, only 50 miles southwest of Craig, in Rio Blanco

County. They killed him and 10 others during what became known as the Meeker Massacre. Terrified white settlers demanded government protection and another treaty was signed in 1880 requiring the Utes to leave Western Colorado and move to a reservation in eastern Utah.

Today, Moffat County is largely supported by energy development including coal mining and natural gas production. Also supporting the economy is ranching and agriculture.

Colorado Encyclopedia. https://coloradoencyclopedia.org/article/moffat-county

Larry: In 1958 we moved to Craig, Colorado, a town about 23 miles west of Mount Harris on Highway US 40, 88 miles to the east of Utah, and 38 miles south of the Wyoming border. The town wasn't a big town then, only about 4,000 people, but it was the largest in Northwest Colorado and the county seat of Moffat County. For us it was the big city.

The major economic activity was farming and ranching and there were also mines in the area. It had a grade school, junior high school and high school, the home of the Moffat County Bull Dogs. Since it was rural and many of the people lived on farms and ranches, many of the kids were bussed in from the surrounding area. There were two main streets, Victory Way, and Yampa Avenue and one stop light where they intersected. Churches were scattered around town of various Protestant denominations, Mormon, Catholic and Greek Orthodox. There was a Greek Orthodox Church in town because of the numbers of Greek sheep ranchers in the county. The town was still small enough that everybody knew everyone else.

When we moved there and built our house at 789 Tucker Street many of the streets were not paved, including our own. It wasn't long before the streets were paved, however, but everyone was required to pay for his portion of the street.

Moving to Craig

Mom in front of Our House at 789 Tucker Street, Craig

Ed: When we lived in Craig my father worked for Walt Caesar in an auto parts store. That didn't last very long so he found a job working for Mildred Watson and Watson Motor Company as an accountant. She had owned it for many, many years.

We lived with my grandmother in the basement of her house while we were having our house built by Uncle Raymond. My uncle was kind of a stubborn fellow and my Dad and Mom wanted a home for my Grandma because she was getting quite elderly. They wanted a mother-in-law apartment on the back of the house. My uncle reduced the size of the apartment by five feet off the original plan for the apartment without my Dad knowing it and it was too late to do anything about it. My Dad was very upset about that.

The lot that my father bought was across the street from the hospital and just a couple of blocks from the park. It was good for me because it was only a block from the elementary school. At that time I went to Breeze Elementary School for 6th grade which had been my Mom's old high school which was later converted into a 6th grade school. Later I went on to junior high school which was just a block up the street and was next to Moffat County High School.

School in Craig

Elementary School - Ed

Ed: After we got the house built I then started kindergarten. In kindergarten I had a teacher named Mrs. Blamey. Her husband had left her and so she was a divorced woman which was quite unusual at the time. I couldn't have asked for a nicer teacher in the world. My first grade teacher was Mrs. Rall.

Larry and Eddie 1966

I'm not sure if she was Miss or Mrs. but she was one tough character. I believe she had come from the Mt. Harris School to Craig to teach first grade and back then there was no flexibility in discipline or academics.

> She said, "Mr. Rutherford what do I see?" and right then I knew I was in big trouble.

A rule was a rule and if you got caught breaking it you were in big trouble. One of the commandments she had was that there was to be no chewing gum in her class. One day, I was outside for recess and I stuck a piece of gum in my mouth, and when I got back in the classroom I had forgotten it was in my mouth. She said, "Mr. Rutherford what do I see?" Right then I knew I was in big trouble. "Could you please come up to the front of the room?" And so I did. And then she said, "Well, there is a consequence for your behavior for not obeying the rules so I want you to come over to this corner." She pulled a stool up to the corner and set me on the stool facing the corner. She pulled a hat out of a cabinet and it was a pointy dunce cap. She stuck that on my head. She said, "Spit out your gum into my hand" and she placed it on my nose. I had to spend the rest of the class day with the gum on my nose staring into the corner. It was not a very comfortable feeling but I learned right then that you, for sure, never chew gum in Mrs. Rall's class.

In second grade I had Mrs. Hladke for my teacher and was a really sweet lady. The other second grade teacher was Mrs. Bersheres. One day I was walking down the hall with a friend and Mike May

> His legs flew out from under him and she dragged him to the principal's office by his hair.

was right in front of me. We were just walking along minding our own business but Mike must have said something to Mrs. Bersheres that she didn't like as she walked past because suddenly I saw her hand reach over me and grab Mike by the hair. His legs flew out from under him and she dragged him to the principal's office by his hair. You can be sure he must have said something very nasty.

Then in third grade my teacher was Miss Spites. I don't know where she came from but she was another tough cookie! That's the first time I had to do a term paper. It had to be ten pages long. I wrote it about trees so now I know the difference between deciduous and coniferous trees. One of the things in her class that was notable was that when the class was noisy she would ring the bell on her desk. Every time she rang the bell it was 15 minutes we would have to stay after class and you had to have a really good reason to leave. She also had a paddle at her desk so after school she would paddle you if you did something wrong.

I remember one time Jennifer Holt was giving a presentation and she asked Miss Spites if she could go to the bathroom first and Miss Spites said, "No, you are just making something up so you don't have to give your presentation." So Jennifer went to the front of the class and she was wearing one of those dresses that flared out. It was starched or pressed so it flared out from her body and she started giving her presentation. When she was giving her presentation I looked up and thought, "That's interesting. There's something coming to the edge of the skirt." She was peeing her pants and it was coming to the edge of the skirt. I can't even remember what happened after that. Maybe Miss Spites said she could go to the bathroom now. But, I know, for sure, it traumatized Jennifer.

I had a good friend then named, Greg McKenna. The McKennas lived right across the alley from us in a shack. The mother was alone raising three kids because the dad ran off. They were very smart kids. The oldest, Steve, went to MIT. Steve was followed by Greg and then the youngest was a girl. I can't remember her name but Greg was the toughest guy you could imagine and just about every day of third grade when the bell rang to go home, he would go out and pound Mike Raily. Mike lived right near us and the McKennas so he would beat the tar out of him along the way. A group of kids would circle up and watch this every day. Finally, Phil Miles, who was the smallest kid in the class, but a bit of a tough kid too, looked at me and said, "I have had enough of this." Before Greg started beating on Mike, Phil went up to him and said, "Greg. This is it. You're done. You're not doing this again." And actually, I don't know why but Greg backed down. He didn't pound on Mike that afternoon and he stopped beating him up after that.

One day Miss Spites told us to bring a picture to school that depicted a family event and then describe it in class. We all brought the picture to school and when she came to Greg he had brought a magazine picture of the Easter parade in New York. While he was talking about it I made the mistake of raising my hand. Miss Spites called on me, "Ed." And I said, "Greg, that is a magazine picture and it has nothing to do with your family. You didn't do that." Well, it was the wrong thing to say and I knew I was in big trouble. After class, I took off running with him in hot pursuit and we got to the hedge that surrounded the hospital that was just across the street from our house. I was only two blocks from the safety of home and I had been running like the dickens. Unfortunately, Greg caught me right at the hedge and I knew it was going to be bad, so I turned around and faced him. He slugged me in the stomach and knocked every bit of air out of me. I thought I can either smile or I can double over and he is going to pummel me even worse. So I started laughing. That must have been humiliating to him

> I thought I can either smile or I can double over and he is going to pummel me even worse

because he took off running home and he didn't continue beating me up.

We set up a baseball diamond and played baseball in a sand lot near the hospital. The custom was that whoever showed up would play baseball. Sometimes, you would have to play both sides of the ball and keep track of your own scores but it was still a lot of fun. If you hit the ball over the hedge, that was a home run. I loved playing baseball.

That was the same year that I decided to somehow get Cheryl McCloud to notice me. One day, she was standing right outside the school grounds on the sidewalk and I was over by the hospital. I told my friend who was with me, "I'm just going to get her attention and she will know I am here." So, I picked up a rock, and I threw it in her direction. I just wanted it to hit close to her. Well, I did get close to her. The curbs were rounded rather than squared off and it hit that curb just the right way that it bounced and hit her right in the forehead. You couldn't have planned it that way. So, I got her attention and it wasn't good.

I had Miss Gibbons for music in the third grade and she assigned me to the trombone. I believe it was that same year that she took me to see "The Music Man." It had just come out and she drove us to the theater. When we came out of the theater after the movie, we looked across at the bank and the bank had the temperature on a lighted sign. It was minus 50 degrees. We walked a block to the car and I was freezing. We got into the car which was one of those old Plymouths where you turn the key and push the button and the button would start the car. So she pushed the button and it was barely turning over. At the same time, I was praying, "Please car, start!" and it did. So we were relieved that we made it home and everything was fine.

In the third grade, a new student, Mary Morris, moved to Craig from Texas. We really weren't used to people coming to town from the outside. Being outside from Texas was even more interesting. She was the toughest kid I had ever met at that time. All the boys would get together to play kick ball or king of the mountain and she just told us, "I'm going to play." She was nice and really good but she was tough and could walk her talk.

One time, Miss Spites rang her bell a couple of times during class so we had about a half an hour to stay after school. During this time we had to be very quiet and could not talk or look around -- just look forward and be totally quiet. And I told Miss Spites, "I can't." She said, "What do you mean, you can't?" I said, "I have to go to religion class tonight." She said, "Would your Mom rather you would be in religion class rather than in time out?" I told her, "My Mom is going to be upset if I don't go to my class." So she said, "OK, you can go to your religion class." I walked down the stairs because we were on the second floor, went out the door and was walking across the playground but sensing that I was being watched. I turned around and Miss Spites had let all the kids come to the window and watch me walk home. That was really humiliating. That sums up the story of third grade.

In fourth grade Mrs. Anderson was my teacher. I had A. Anderson but there was also an L. Anderson. My teacher was quite an elderly lady and she had narcolepsy. It was strange because I would ask her a question and she would say, "Come up to my desk." One time when I got up to her desk, she was already fast asleep, I guess. I stood there and I didn't know what to do. The kids started laughing and finally she heard them, woke up and said, "Thank you for coming up." I thought that was pretty peculiar. She didn't even know she had fallen asleep. She was a very lovely lady all the same.

In fifth grade I had Mrs. L. Anderson and Mr. Bridges. They taught as a team. L. Anderson was a red-headed lady who was feisty and tough. Mr. Bridges was a nice guy but he was also very demanding. What I remember about fifth grade that was particularly memorable was one time Mr. Bridges was teaching a class and needed to leave the classroom. He told us, "I gave you an assignment, I want you to work. I don't want you talking or looking around. Just keep working on the assignment and I will be back in about ten or fifteen minutes." So as soon as he left the room, of course, I started talking with the people in the desks around me. I didn't see him come back in but I saw the terror on the faces of the kids I was chit-chatting with. He grabbed a roll of duct tape and before I could even do anything, he had it over my head and around my head

> **He grabbed a roll of duct tape and before I could even do anything, he had it over my head and around my head three times.**

151

three times where I could just breath through my nose and he said to me, 'There, Mr. Rutherford, you will wear this the entire day and you can only take it off when you leave for the day." So here I was taped up for the whole class. At the end of the day, I left and didn't realize that the tape was attached to my hair. When I took the tape off, it really hurt. I'm sure he got a good laugh about that.

L. Anderson was very difficult but was still very sympathetic to the kids. She knew I understood math quite well so she talked to me about helping Mike May, the guy who got dragged down the hall in second grade. He was having a hard time so she took his desk and put him out in the hall. She told me, "Mr. Rutherford, I want you to teach Mr. May math and however you do that is fine, but you have to give him some special time and show him how to do these problems." So I worked with him and I don't know how good I was but it worked out well for him.

Then, at the end of the fifth grade, I was once again infatuated with Cheryl McCloud. I asked her if she would want to go get a tennis racquet and play tennis with me. I remember getting it all set up and running across the street toward the hospital. I was going to meet her near the empty lot where we played baseball. I was so elated and was thinking I was so cool that I closed my eyes for a couple of seconds while I was running.

> In my ecstasy, I ran right into a post that had a big bolt sticking out of it.

In my ecstasy, I ran right into a post that had a big bolt sticking out of it. It tore right down my face and cut me wide open. I was stunned. I turned around and raced back to the house. Mom and Dad were both gone but grandma was there. Grandma was 81 or 82 at the time and she was smart, she was very smart. She had a lot of home remedies for these problems. She went to the garage to get something for me. I guess she had called my Dad, but in the meantime she came back from the garage with a can of turpentine. She said, "This is going to hurt Sweetie. Tilt your head back." She had a towel and she poured that turpentine through that open wound. It stung like the dickens! Then Dad got home and took me over to the hospital and Dr. Thurston sewed me up. Dad was so good. He stayed right by my side the whole time and Dr. Thurston thought that I was in pretty good humor considering I had my face ripped up. He said, "Hmm, this wound is pretty clean. How did that happen?" I told him, "Well, my grandmother poured turpentine through it." "Pretty smart grandmother," he said. "She really flushed out all the dirt and whatever bacteria there was. It was pretty clean."

In sixth grade Mrs. Driscol was my teacher. She gave me the first introduction I had to socialism. She said some of the most ridiculous things. She told us, for example, that the cocoa bean had all these pieces of insect wings in it. Sometimes it was an interesting class but I still didn't get much out of it other than that.

One day, Larry Roundtree and another kid were chasing me. I said something to him he didn't like so he ran me down and

> **He chased me down and made me eat grass as fast as he could pull it out of the ground.**

made me eat grass as fast as he could pull out of the ground. He had

153

me backed flat on the ground and he was stuffing grass in my mouth and there wasn't anything I could do about it. We actually became pretty good friends after that. I don't know how that works.

I got glasses that year. I had been a pretty good basketball player in sixth grade. I don't know if it was the glasses or self-image or having my face all cut up but I just wasn't very good any more.

Seventh grade was the first year of junior high school because we had seventh, eighth and ninth all in junior high. It was a good time. Can't remember if it was seventh or eighth grade but they had the mock elections and, of course, we had to act it out. We had the standard Democrat and Republican running but there was also a guy named Pat Paulson in the race. I was designated as Pat Paulson, a comedy actor, and I had to "perform" in front of everybody. It was kind of embarrassing.

That year, the teachers played ping pong with us at lunchtime about every day. That was a lot of fun.

In eighth grade there wasn't much going on worth relating. In the ninth grade, however, there was Mr. Rowe. Mr. Rowe was one intimidating guy. He was our typing instructor. I remember he was also an *Outward Bound* coach. One day, he put up a video that we were supposed to watch. He told us there was to be no talking and we were just to watch the video and then he left the room. He came back and I heard all this commotion behind me. He had grabbed Dan Boscha who was sitting in the desk behind me. He had him in a vice grip by the shoulders and dragged him out to the hall overturning the desk because Dan was not paying attention to the movie. He made the mistake of writing something or doing other homework. He threw him up against the wall three times so hard it made the room shake. It got people's attention.

> Mr. Hopoley emerged from his office carrying a ¾ in lead pipe at least a foot to 18 in long.

Ninth grade was interesting, too, because Mr. Hopoley was the physical education teacher and one of his students, Melvin Culverwell, was a rowdy, mean kind of a guy. The day before the last day of school Melvin told me, "I'm going to beat Mr. Hopoley up the last day of school." So he came to school and was ready to beat him up when Mr. Hopoley emerged from his office carrying a ¾ in. lead pipe at least a foot to 18 in. long. He was whacking it on his hand saying, "If any of you boys think you are big enough to take me out, I'll use this lead pipe to beat the tar out of you." So Melvin chose not to go after him that day after all.

High School – Ed

Ed: High school was an exciting time for me. I was in band and had started that in second grade. It was in third grade that Miss Gibbons assigned me to the trombone. I loved it. But going into high school was a whole different thing from Junior high. I wasn't one who studied really hard and I mowed lawns in the summer. I couldn't play sports until my junior year and so I decided that I wanted to play football instead of cut grass. I sold my lawn business that had been my brother's originally and played football. I started out as a receiver and then went on to tackle on offence and guard on defense.

The coaches were, I would say, appropriately hard. I remember an event after a very bad loss one weekend. We weren't doing all that great. I think we had only won one game that year. So Monday came around for football practice. The coaches started doing the whistle drill where every time they whistled, you changed what you were doing and started doing something else.

You got down on all fours and when they whistled, you started running; or you dropped to the ground and walked like a crab with your arms and your legs pulling you along the ground; or you would roll over and jump up and start running again back and forth and so on. Mr. Tonso was our coach and Mr. Irvin was doing the whistle drill and he just kept going on and on. It became dark so they pulled cars up and turned the lights on so we could see what we were doing. Mr. Irvin kept us going for probably another hour. We did this for about three hours and people were throwing up and passing out on the field. It was unbelievable. Fortunately, Mr. Tonso, who was the head coach, finally came over and said, "Daryl (Irvin) that's enough. You have to let them go." He released us, and I'll tell you what, we and we hustled double time back to the locker room.

> People were throwing up and passing out on the field.

We played in Steamboat Springs one year. We alternated home games so Steamboat would play in Craig and then Craig would go to Steamboat the next year. This year, we got there and they were actually plowing snow off of the field. There was a lot of snow, maybe a foot to 18 inches so they had to plow the snow off so we could play the game. There were no spectators. The temperature was minus 10 to minus 15 degrees below zero outside. Of course, you didn't

> They were actually plowing snow off the field so we could play the game.

have coats at the time and so you had to jog in place to keep warm and to keep your toes from freezing. That was a pretty miserable night.

Mr Jepkema, probably the best teacher in the high school, taught me math and pre-calculus. He had a big moustache that was curled at the ends. I remember once, he gave us an assignment to do in class. He said, "Mr. Rutherford why aren't you doing your assignment?" I said, "I forgot my pencil." He said, "Where might your pencil be?" I said, "It's at home, Mr. Jepkema, I left it at home." So he said, "You better go home and get it." So, I got up, went home, retrieved my pencil and came back. It only took 10-15 minutes. I went up to him and he said, "Where do you think you're going?" "I got my pencil, I'm going to sit down." "You're tardy. You have to go to the principal's office." That was a funny experience. If you want to make a point in a class, don't forget your pencil. I never forgot it again.

I was pretty close to my band teacher, Mr. Davis. I was in advanced band. He let me conduct for one of the pieces in a concert and I just loved it. He said, "Ed, you're a natural at this." And I did really feel like a natural at it.

I was walking down the hall one day at school and I looked into a classroom and Mrs. Olson was there crying at her desk. I went in and asked her what was wrong. She said, "My husband and I are having trouble." Now this was a very awkward situation because her husband was one of the other teachers in the school. She

> I looked into a classroom and Mrs. Olson was there crying at her desk.

was telling this to a student. That being said, I asked her what the problem was. "Well, when we got married, we had an agreement that we wouldn't have any children." She said, "I changed my mind and I want children, but he reminded me that

I agreed to never have children. It's a big problem." Oh, my gosh, that was a **big problem**.

Edward - 1970

High school was a fascinating time. I remember at Homecoming each class would create a float. The juniors would design a float and the seniors would also build a float. I recall when I was a junior, I had borrowed my brother's car, a cherry red 1962 Ford Galaxy 500. I drove to the place where we were putting together the float and, all of a sudden, here came the seniors. They planned to mess up our float and cause us trouble. The float was in a storage barn with a huge garage door at one end. They were trying to get in and we were trying to keep them out. Tina Clifton, who was a senior, stuck her toes underneath the door and was trying to lift it up. And I think it was Mary Morris who went to get a sledge hammer. She didn't hammer on Tina's toes but she just dropped the end on her toe and broke it. That really incited trouble! The seniors took off and came back with a bunch of eggs and, unfortunately, they aimed at my brother's car. He wasn't real happy about that.

One story illustrates the type of discipline we had even in high school. We had a Physical Education instructor named Mr. Brown. He was an ex-football player and he weighed about 240 pounds. He was a very strong man, a Mormon and very much a disciplinarian. Kim Steele and I went into the locker room and, of course, everyone was required to shower.

When I was showering I had soap on my face and around my eyes so I had closed them. Kim Steele grabbed the hose that was used to clean the shower. He turned the hot water on and sprayed it around my behind. It just burned the tar out of me. I got so mad I got a bar of soap and heaved it at him hitting him in the shin. It was really painful. To retaliate, he flew after me through one of the doorways on each side of the shower, back into the dressing room and then back out the other door.

While I was running around I stopped, grabbed the hose and waited for Kim to come around the corner. When I heard someone coming, I turned the hose on and I sprayed Mr. Brown instead. Well that was a big mistake! Mr. Brown said, "Boys, you and Kim, go into my office. Now!" I said, "Yeah, yeah. I'll just put on my clothes and be right in." "Uh, uh. You mess around in the nude, you get punished in the nude." So Kim and I went into his office and he said, "Grab my desk, boys." So we leaned over his desk and he brought out this board about 14 inches long, 6 inches wide and a half inch thick. He took that board back as far as he could and he came into us and nearly drove us over the desk. It was so unbelievably painful! So we limped back into the locker room.

> So we leaned over his desk and he brought out this board about 14 inches long, 6 inches wide and a half inch thick.

It was dead silence in there. The boys were dressing but no one said a word. One of the guys came up to me and whispered, "Ed, your cheeks are bright red and there is a white spot right in the middle. He must have really whacked you!" "Yeah, he hit me really hard!!" So you didn't mess around with Mr. Brown!

School – Larry

Larry: I really don't remember a whole lot about my life in school. I attended junior high school in an old brick building across from the Catholic Church. Mrs. Hall was my science and math teacher there. I particularly remember the projects that we made in her class, all of which were built from scratch. I found the electric motor, electro magnet and the radio fascinating to build and operate.

Miss Potter taught English and was a very hard taskmistress. I don't know how old she was but she had white hair and was a spinster. There really weren't a lot of smiles and laughter in that class, only business. God help you if you forgot your assignment or anything, for that matter, that was necessary for the class. She made sure you regretted the error. Being such brilliant kids, however, we got sick of her class and decided that we should all sign a petition to give to the principal asking for her to be fired. That was a big mistake. Not only was she not fired but we had to apologize to her. Sadly, she really was hurt by the whole episode. I really am sorry I ever participated in that mean scheme.

> Being such brilliant kids, we decided to give the principal a petition to have our teacher fired.

Sometime during junior high we all had to take a class called Health and Hygiene. Actually, it really was about things like cleanliness, bacteria, diseases and such. But one session was for "sex education." The boys and the girls were separated into different rooms with a female teacher explaining it to the girls and a male teacher explaining it to the boys. It was a little embarrassing but really, it was little more than explaining sexual plumbing with minimal detail and some charts. Most of it was no news to anyone.

There was a kitchen in the building but I don't think there was a cafeteria. Most kids just went home for lunch. Our house was only four blocks away so taking a lunch to school was unnecessary. Physical Education took place in the gym and out on the baseball field. I was never particularly apt at any of it so it was more pain than fun. I was always one of the last to be picked for team sports. But that's OK. There was no lasting psychological damage and I really didn't care all that much about it all.

MCHS Prom King and Queen c.1965

There were a few notable classes and teachers in high school. The math, algebra and calculus teacher was a young fellow, Mr. Cook. He had a flattop haircut and always wore a white shirt with a skinny dark tie. He used an overhead projector more than a black board and wrote on sheets of plastic placed on the projector. He was brilliant! He could write and solve formulas fast as lightning with his eyes closed. I never really understood all the math as an integral part of my psyche. I got good grades in his class but it was with so much difficulty it felt like I was frying my brains.

By my senior year I had taken all my mandatory "college" classes so I had electives to select. I had an "Individual Studies" class where a student selected the subject. I chose engineering drawing and aviation because I thought I wanted to be a pilot at the time. I really don't remember what in blazes I did to satisfy the requirements for the course but I got an A in it. I also took a choir class. That really was something I learned that lasted a lifetime. Mr. Dennis Kettle was the teacher. He was newly out of college so he wasn't much older than the students. That would have been fine, but there were a few guys that got into the

Moffat County High School c. 1965

class just because it filled a credit to graduate and they didn't want to take "shop." They mostly thought it was it big joke. Mr. Kettle was a very good teacher but in exasperation with some of the behavior and the quality of the singing, he would break pencils in half and throw them across the room. Nevertheless, we sang some great music and did it quite well. We sang parts of Handel's *Messiah*, classical polyphony and great secular choral works. I really enjoyed the choir and was reasonably accomplished at singing. I was in the Select Choir and qualified as an alternate to All State Choir. I was also in the parish choir and we sang Gregorian chant, traditional hymns and some polyphony. Not bad for a small rural parish.

> **He would break pencils in half and throw them across the room.**

I also took engineering drawing. That too, was a skill that was valuable in college and really ever since from time to time. I loved the detail and the precision that was demanded by the teacher. Not even a 32nd of an inch of line could be out of place.

All stray marks and lines were scrutinized and duly noted. Creating an image using a T-square, triangles, protractors and other mechanical tools was very satisfying and fascinating for me.

I liked to play basketball even though I wasn't very good at it. I "played" on the junior varsity team for two years, as I recall. But I probably only was in a game for the combined time of five minutes. That's OK, you can't mess up too much on the bench. I came back for more the next year and the only notable thing I did was break one of the star player's feet during practice. I was blocking him as he went up for a layup and came down on his foot. He was out for the season. I can tell you that wasn't a way to win a popularity contest in the school. I concluded that sports weren't a productive way to spend my time.

> I came back for more the next year and the only notable thing I did was break one of the star player's feet during practice.

Instead, I got involved in other school activities. I was in the Science Club and Editor of the annual, for example. I actually designed all the graphics and illustrations for the Moffat County High School Annual of 1965. I was also in the Latin Club. I don't remember anything about what we did in the club except for the Latin Club party. Everyone dressed up in togas, mostly. Mom, however, actually made a Roman soldier costume for me, including the helmet. She was a remarkable seamstress. The armor was made out of glossy gray fabric that resembled metal and I carved an "authentic" two edged sword. Maybe we just sat around, ate grapes and quoted Caesar's *Gallic wars* in Latin or something. Whatever we did, however, it was entertaining.

Mr. Medina taught Russian and Spanish. I decided that Russian would be a good language to know for the time. Mr. Medina was pretty laid back in the Russian class and, sadly, didn't demand very much. I'm sure he was more engaged in his Spanish classes since that was his first speaking language. Besides, he didn't do anything about the girl in the class that always wore a super short mini skirt and was a huge distraction. The only Russian I remember is, "Здрáвствуйте. Как вáши делá? Спаси́бо, хорошó. Как у вас?" Or something like that. Not terribly useful, but I got an "A" in the class.

By some fluke, I was elected treasurer of the senior class and I was shocked when at graduation I was given the Outstanding Senior Boy award. The selection was made by nominations from the faculty. I guess I didn't cause anyone any problems while in school.

Life in Town

Dragging Main

Ed: We would drag main, Victory Way in Craig, and pick up girls. We would go back and forth and up and down the streets. All of a sudden somebody said let's go to the Midwest Café and we would go there for drinks, talk and just hang out. But nobody was really out of control as I recall. We were having just a pretty good time and for the most part didn't bother anyone else.

Sherwood Forest

Larry: We lived about a block from Fortification Creek which ran though the east side of Craig. There was a green space between the creek and any homes. All along the west side of the creek were huge cottonwood trees with a thick undergrowth of grass and bushes. The kids in the neighborhood dubbed it Sherwood Forest. There was a natural trail that ran along the bank from the park to about a mile north and it was a lot of fun to ride a bike on because it had lots of ups and downs along the way. When the water was low later on in the summer we would catch

Larry on a Bicycle

frogs and minnows in the creek. The boys spent a lot of time there.

Ed: When we moved to Craig I was a little boy and there was a place we called Sherwood Forest just a couple of blocks from the house. We would go in there and have all kinds of games like cowboys and Indians, etc. My brother was always very creative so he decided to dig out this hole in Sherwood Forest and cover it with branches and leaves and that would be our fort. I thought that was the coolest place in the world then.

We also had big family picnics in the nearby city park and there would be 40 or 50 people from the Knez family and sometimes the Rutherfords would join us. They were huge get-togethers and everyone had a really great time.

Dorothy and Joe Rotter

Ed: Dorothy and Joe Rotter lived in the basement of our house in an apartment. Dorothy loved being with people, especially Mom. Some days, she would stay longer than was expected and Mom would have to find a polite way to ask her to leave. That was sometimes difficult for our family but, nevertheless, Dorothy

Dorothy and Joe Rotter, Mom and Dad, Eddie, Grandma Knez and Larry

became like an aunt to me. She was just a good person and Joe was too.

Larry: Dorothy didn't like to be in the basement because she was terrified of there being a fire and her not being able to get out. I can understand that. There was only one exit from the apartment as the windows were quite small and high on the wall. We also kept a barrel of gasoline in the garage for the lawn mowers. That probably didn't help.

The Church Next Door

Larry: Our house in Craig was across from the Memorial Hospital with an Assembly of God Church next door and a Church of the Nazarene across the street to the North. The services of the Assembly of God were quite a novelty for us Catholics. It seemed like a large portion of the service involved weeping and moaning that we could hear even inside our house. Of course, there was a lot of singing, too, and the preacher was loud enough to hear but not loud enough to understand.

Mom worked at the hospital for a while to help put kids through college. She was a cook in the hospital kitchen and the kitchen faced our house. It was pretty easy to keep us boys under surveillance from that vantage point.

St. Michael's Parish

Larry: When we got to Craig I was trained as an altar boy and served frequently at Sunday Mass and regularly during the week before school began. If there was a funeral that needed an altar boy, we were excused from school so we could be at the service.

St. Michael's Church was about 50 years old at the time and had the sacristy on one side and the altar boy's vestry on the other joined by a very narrow hallway behind the altar. I was very serious on and around the altar but my friend Roger Hutton who was also a server tended to be quite talkative. One time before Mass he continued to talk and talk while we were putting our cassocks on. I was sure people in the congregation could hear and I had had enough. I tried to shush him to no avail so I decided to give him a push to get his attention. It did, and he shoved back. In short order, our fists were flying but, fortunately, nothing connected. No doubt the scuffle was heard in the church but, thankfully, no one said anything.

> In short order, our fists were flying but, fortunately, nothing connected.

Ed: When we moved to Craig Father Syrianey was the pastor. He was followed by Fathers Anderson, Fraszcowski, Lievens and Father John. Larry was an altar boy for Fr. Anderson. I was an altar boy for Fr. Fraszkowski. He would have ice cream socials for the boys and would fill a huge mixing bowl full of it for us. He was just super!

Fr. Levins was a very outgoing man. He had been in the navy for eight years and he became a priest later in life. He was quite wealthy personally and he was able to do a lot of different things. He would come down to the tennis courts to play a match with us. Father, Mark Lochran, Dad and I would play tennis together regularly. Mark was from Montana, and his aunt (Mrs. Conway) was my Mom's boss at the hospital. Mark had a habit of swinging just as hard as he could at the ball and one time he really slammed it. Father Levins was playing up at the net and he hit Father right in the forehead. I thought it had knocked him out. He kind of staggered a little bit but finally regained his footing. It was kind of a funny sight and Father Levins took it pretty well. Father also drove an Audi at the time. There wasn't even another Audi in all of Craig. He just swore (figuratively) by Audi cars saying they were the best car ever made. All the priests we knew in Craig were really good people.

Learning to Drive – The Hard Way

Larry: All our cousins on their farms learned to drive at a very young age so it came natural to them but I had no experience driving. One day, we were out driving in a field on the Antone Knez property. They decided it would be a good time to teach me how to drive. I had never been behind the wheel before but it seemed safe enough being in the middle of the field in a pickup. I sat in the driver's seat and got a quick driver's briefing. So I turned on the engine, put the truck in gear, let out on the clutch and pushed down on the gas. Off we went but how do you stop this thing? We were rolling full speed downhill heading toward the fence and a deep ditch. Now there was panic in the cab with kids shouting to push in the clutch and step on the brake. Finally, I pressed the brake hard enough to stall the engine. Everyone breathed a sigh of relief as it jerked to a stop.

Flower Garden and Grotto

Flower Garden and Grotto

Larry: I always had an inclination toward gardening but we didn't have space for a vegetable garden. Aunt Louise always grew vegetables across the alley on Rose Street, though. I got a wild idea that it would be nice to have a Mary garden with a fountain, small pool and lots of flowers. Dad was always a good sport in helping out with these projects. We poured a concrete stand for an outdoor statue of the Blessed Virgin. It had a basin in front of the statue with a tube up from the middle that shot water into the air a short way with the water running over the edge of the basin. We also built a concrete pool about four feet by four feet and a foot deep that the stand, basin and statue stood in. A pump took the water from the pool, up through the stand and into the basin. The garden was enclosed with a fence and a red rock circular path surrounded the fountain. Flower beds surrounded the path and were filled with gladiolas, chrysanthemums and cosmos. I believe Mom did most of the planting. It really was beautiful.

Building and making things

Larry: I enjoyed building and making things. In one small room in the basement, I had my electric trains going around the room on wide shelves and powered by four transformers set in a control panel that controlled four separate sections of the track. A bridge crossed the doorway and I built a lighted coal tipple. I had two trains that ran around the room. One was given to me at Christmas when we lived in Mt. Harris and the other I bought from a friend.

Go-karts were very popular when I was in junior high school but we could never afford to buy one. I decided I would l make my own so I designed a body frame and Dad had it welded out of one inch tubing. I used the wheels off the mail cart that Dad had on the one he built in Mt. Harris. I found a gasoline motor that was used on an old washing machine and fashioned a steering wheel that turned the front wheels with rope and pulleys. The frame was covered with quarter-inch plywood and painted red and white. It had a chrome grill from an old Ford Falcon. It was pretty impressive. The engine was on the back and drove one wheel with a pulley and belt. It looked great and, in concept, it should have worked. Unfortunately, the engine didn't have enough power to actually make it go. It turned out to be a no-go kart.

I really liked sailing-ship stories and the romance of sailing the ocean. I decided I would make my own sailing ship out of a 30 in by 10 in by 8 in piece of wood I found. I carved that wood into the hull of the ship and then added three masts about 18 in. tall with all the rigging and sails. Each side had ten or so cannons protruding from the sides made from hollow curtain rods. It was fun to stuff the cannons with matchbook match heads and light them to produce the effect of cannon fire. Later, I decided to add a rudder operated by electromagnets. It worked fine on land but the control wires couldn't be very long and when I put it on the lake the wires produced too much drag so the rudder was ineffective.

I never was discouraged with failed projects, however. Another time I decided to build a raft that I could take down Fortification Creek in the spring. I put several logs together on our property and even made a mast and sail for the raft. There was one problem, however. It was too heavy to move to the creek.

I had better luck making rubber band guns of various sizes and types. Some had multiple clothes pin triggers. Others were single-shot pistols. A more elaborate rifle had a carved gun stock but it was actually a sling shot operated by a trigger. That worked pretty well too and was a fun project.

In addition to rubber band gun fights, Ed and I had armies of lead "soldiers." We couldn't get actual lead soldiers that looked like army men so we found a couple of bullet molds that Grandpa Knez had owned. These slugs were enormous! They were about an inch long and nearly a half an inch in diameter. Outside of town was a firing range where the targets were backed up against some tall sand rock cliffs. A lot of the time people would just shoot at the sand rocks and the lead

> **I probably had some brain damage handling all that lead so frequently.**

would drop to the ground below. We would gather all this lead and then melt it in a tin can on the kitchen stove and pour it into the molds. We made dozens of these soldiers. Ed and I would line them up in ranks facing each other and roll large "steelies" at them until one side or the other had knocked them all down. I probably had some brain damage handling all that lead so frequently. You would likely have to use a hazmat suit to touch them now.

I won't even go into my failed attempt to build a four-foot-long rocket.

Boy Scouts

Roger Hutton, Fr. Fraczkowski, Larry
Ad Altare Dei Award

Larry: I was in the Boy Scouts for several years. I didn't start in Cub Scouts. I'm not sure there was a Cub Scout pack in town. The principal of the junior high, Mr. Turner, was the scout master. He must have been in the army at some time because part of the scout meeting started with marching drills. We all had walking sticks (guns) that we painted and put designs on. I'm not sure what rank I achieved. Maybe only First Class but possibly Star.

I enjoyed scouts very much and went to scout camp outside of Denver at least once. There I earned the Mile Swim Badge by swimming back and forth in the lake there accompanied by scouts in a row boat. I also earned the scout Freeze Out badge by sleeping overnight in a pup tent outside in the snow on Uncle

Antone's property. I was also awarded the Catholic *Ad Altare Dei* medal and it was presented to scouts at a ceremony at the cathedral in Denver. That was a really big deal!

The scout hut was in the city park. It was a really nice large log cabin only three blocks from home.

Driving to Wyoming

Larry: One summer late at night, I couldn't sleep. I must have been concerned about going into the Air Force and getting married in the not too distant future. After tossing and turning in bed for a while, I decided that I might be able to sleep if I took a short drive in the country. It was the middle of the night so there was no one on the streets. I thought I would just drive a few miles up the road toward Wyoming. There was no one on that road either. It was a clear, starry night so it was beautiful out. I got as far as the turn-off to Black Mountain when I decided to turn around. I pulled off onto a side road and was planning to back out and head south. The engine died and to my horror, I couldn't get it started again. The battery was dead.

It was a cold night out and I had just put my shoes on but was still in my pajamas. I tried to build a little fire alongside the road but I only had two matches and all the tinder was damp. Both attempts failed. Mom and Dad, of course, would have no idea where I had gone and they wouldn't find out until morning. There were no ranch houses for miles around.

> I tried to build a little fire alongside the road but all I had was two matches and all the tinder was damp.

Finally a car was coming down the road. I was saved! The guy stopped for me and I explained that I tried to turn around to go back to Craig but the battery in the pickup was dead. He said he would take me home and he didn't ask any questions and I didn't really want to talk about it either. I don't remember what Dad and Mom said but they should have said it was a really stupid thing to do.

Tragic Event

Ed: Sometimes my cousins were a little bit wild. One cousin got into a car accident where the driver was drunk. They had been drinking in Hayden and were on their way back to Craig. Another cousin, was also in the car. And a third younger brother, was with them but refused to get in the car at Hayden. They were in a powder blue 1964 convertible Mercury. They were going pretty fast and passed a car going over the rise of a hill. They hit an oncoming car and killed a family of five. The driver of the Mercury was also killed. He was thrown several yards down the middle of the road. The older cousins survived, but it was a terrible event.

Even though most of life in those days in our small town seemed ideal, sadly, there was a tacit acceptance of drinking and alcoholism. In some cases, this part of life caused considerable heartache and conflict within marriages and families, and in the above case and other similar events, tragic loss of life and misery for some.

Winter in Craig

*Winter came down to our home one night
Quietly pirouetting on silver-toed slippers of snow
And we, we were children once again.* – **Bill Morgan, Jr.**

Larry: We spent a lot of time in the snow maybe because there was snow a lot of the time. Behind the sand rocks on the north side of Craig there was a sledding/skiing hill that even had a rope tow. That was fun and was very cheap entertainment. When I was in high school I designed a bob sled and Dad had it built in a welding shop. It seated about seven riders, had a brake on the back and the front section of the runners pivoted under the driver using handle bars. Down the center was a two-by-ten plank painted red and the riders put their feet on foot rests along the side above the runners. It was very heavy but it did move fast on the right hill.

The Buck Peak Incident

Larry: Buck Peak was one of those hills. The "peak" was a high hill south of the Fedinic ranch and had an oil well at the top. The road was winding and kept clear for the oil company trucks that regularly serviced the well. The snow was packed nicely and made a great sledding hill as there was little traffic, none at night. Some of us high school guys would like to go out there at night and build a bonfire at the top. We would take turns sledding while one person would drive the car and/or pickup truck to the bottom to pick up the sledders and sleds. One night we all gathered at the top of the hill and my friend Mike Chivington was the designated driver. He proceeded down the hill in my 1954 Buick and we were following shortly behind on the bob sled. We were sailing down the road with the sled skidding around the corners when shortly we passed Mike standing forlornly along the road. He wasn't supposed to be there. With much difficulty we brought the sled to a stop and walked back to see what was up. Well what was up was down. The car had gone over the edge out of sight from the road and settled in the deep snow and scrub oak bushes. How would we ever get it out?

> Mike stood forlornly along the road. He wasn't supposed to be there!

One person had a small jeep there with a winch in front. We tried to drag the car out of the snow. It was a great idea but the car was so heavy that the winch only pulled the jeep to the edge of the precipice. I had no choice but to call Dad and ask for help. We had to go over to Uncle Charlie and Aunt Louise's farm house to call. Dad worked at the local Ford dealer and they had a tow truck. He came out with the tow truck but it was very tricky because the road was narrow, the car was heavy and it had to be lifted virtually straight up and dragged onto the road. We got it out and surprisingly, because of the deep snow, the car was undamaged.

A Toboggan Story

Ed: Another winter activity we liked to do was riding a toboggan in the snow. We would go up to my Uncle Charlie's (Fedinic) and toboggan down a slope in a field. He had a field very close to the house which was quite steep. You had to walk to the top pulling the toboggan. Then everyone would get on the toboggan, sail down the hill and go flying over the road. One time we went out there, a bunch of my cousins, Tommy, Leon, Ralph, me. We got on at the top and started down. It went faster and faster as it picked up speed. We were going so fast, and it was scary, scary, scary!

> All I heard was, "Eddie, Eddie, Eddie. Eddie where are you?" They found my hat but they couldn't find me.

All of a sudden we hit deep snow and the snow came flying over the front and we couldn't see where we were going. We jumped over a high bank along the road and became airborne. Everyone went flying off the toboggan when we hit the ground. My cousins started looking for me. All I heard was, "Eddie, Eddie, Eddie. Eddie where are you?" I was about a foot under the snow. They found my hat but they couldn't find me. It was actually pretty funny! Larry was there too and thought he had broken his back, anyway it hurt badly enough.

My brother was very creative and would make various art projects. One year he decided to make the Statue of Liberty in the snow right next to our house. So, with him as the director, we all worked on it. I think he had some kind of a wooden frame supporting it. It was so realistic everyone in the neighborhood was coming over to help when he was putting it together. It was probably over ten feet tall. It was quite a deal. There even was a picture of it in the Craig newspaper after we were done. It was very impressive!

Ed: Another fun thing we did in the winter was snowmobiling. I got my Dad to go in with me to buy a snowmobile. I'm not sure if I paid for it or if we paid half each but we both loved it. It was a wide-belt Ski-Doo brand and we would go out to my Uncle Antone's and run the snowmobile around the hills, fields and roads in the winter. It was just a blast! I remember once, though, my Aunt Cleo talked my Mom into snowmobiling with her. They were on my aunt's snowmobile coming down the road and we were standing out there watching an impending disaster. All of a sudden we heard my Mom screaming, "It won't stop! It won't stop!" Aunt Cleo shouts, "Let up on the gas!" "I did and it won't stop!" They came around the corner and they ran right into the rock wall that was in front of my aunt's house. The crash threw my Mom's back out and she almost had to be carried off the snowmobile into the house. Aunt Cleo was concerned about her but later she had a good laugh about the event.

Statue of Liberty with Larry and Friends

Buck Peak – Fun Times

Ed: In the winter when we were older especially, we would go up to Buck Peak. My brother Larry, made a bobsled that held, I think, seven guys. One time we put it on a road up there that was a mile long. You could actually sled for a mile! It was solid ice at the top so you would get going extremely fast. We loaded that sled up and I was the little guy on the sled. My brother and friends were all in college at the time and they had come for the holidays. We pushed off and went speeding down the road. We got to about the second turn and the bobsled just went flying and I went flying, too. All the other guys were thrown through the air and were rolling down the road. It is a wonder no one got hurt badly.

Toboggan Crash on Buck Peak

Ed: My cousin Delores thought she and her friend would take a toboggan down the Buck Peak road which had a lot of sharp S turns. They all got on that toboggan and pushed off. After the first corner they lost it right into the trees. She broke an arm and I don't know who else was hurt but they were probably going 40-50 mph when they went over the edge and ran right into a tree. In another event, my other cousin Loretta and some friends went up on Howleson Hill in Steamboat Springs. They thought it would be a fun thing to take a toboggan off the ski jump. Imagine that! There were four or five riders on it. Two of them were hurt seriously from that. What a ride that was!!

Larry, Dad, Ralph Henderson, Christy Camilletti and Eddie

Lost in a Blizzard

Barbara: It was October, 1961. Marlene and Ralph had been married two months. They decided to go hunting about noon and left Craig with two apples and two candy bars for lunch. "We were 19 years old", said Marlene. They told everyone they were going out to hunt west of Craig. It was very warm and they were dressed lightly. Marlene wore tennis shoes. When they didn't see any deer or elk west of Craig, they decided to drive to Strawberry/California Park north of Hayden.

They were driving a four wheel drive pickup. There was a plastic tarp in the back. As they drove higher and higher, they saw they were getting into deeper and deeper snow. They also noticed their gas supply was dwindling. Ralph thought they could continue on the road and reach Hayden to get gas.

As they drove along, they noticed a forest ranger cabin by the road and commented that they could probably stay there if the conditions got worse. It did get worse and they high centered about one mile past the cabin. By that time, it was dark and they knew they had to stay overnight in the pickup. They got the plastic tarp to cover themselves and then ran the truck a few minutes every half an hour to warm the cab a bit. They also heard the radio reports asking anyone with news about Marlene and Ralph Henderson to report it to the sheriff's office because their parents were worried about them.

> They got the plastic tarp to cover themselves and then ran the truck a few minutes to warm the cab a bit.

When daylight came, they knew they had to get back to the cabin. The snow was knee deep. It took them a long time to walk the mile and they thought they were freezing. They had to wade through a stream but finally made it to the cabin where Ralph broke the lock. Marlene said it was exhausting to walk through snow that deep.

The cabin was well equipped with food and wood for a fire. They heated up some canned soup. They could hear a plane above so went out in the snow and stomped out SOS in the field in front of the cabin. A second plane came by and the pilot realized that they were there. A note was dropped to them saying that the rescuers would be on their way. The sheriff (who was staying with a dying father) came to get them and he was not happy. He scolded them the entire trip back to Craig. They were told that thirteen search and rescue planes from Grand Junction had been in the air looking for them. Most planes were searching in the area west of Craig since that's where they said they would be.

The thought by those back home in Craig was that they had had a car accident. It was only "accidental" that one plane decided to go over Strawberry Park. (Surely, it was Mom and Dad's prayers). Both sets of parents were very happy to see them but Ralph's Dad let them know how stupid they were to try to drive around the mountains in a snow storm.

Larry: On Thanksgiving of my junior year I asked Fran if she would like to spend Thanksgiving break at our house. We had just been engaged in October and I wanted her to spend the holiday at my home. It was a very nice visit but when we started back to the university Sunday afternoon there were a few snowflakes in the air and by the time we reached Steamboat Springs, it was snowing hard. That didn't deter me, however. We were accustomed to driving in the snow. We were in the Ford Galaxy and we started up Rabbit Ears Pass.

> **As we went around the curve, the car started sliding toward the edge.**

It just got worse and worse as we climbed and neared the summit. Just before we reached it, there was a long curve so the pavement banked slightly to the inside. As we went around the curve, the car started sliding toward the edge. I backed up twice to try again and each time the car slid toward the edge. Finally, we went back down the pass toward Steamboat to the nearest gas station and had chains put on the car. It never occurred to me that we should go home and wait till the next day.

So we got the chains on and there were no more problems sliding or being stalled on the road but we were only able to go 30 – 35 mph with the chains on. There were only 188 miles to go through Walden, over Snowy Range in Wyoming (the name should be a warning) and through Laramie. There was so much blowing snow that we had to just follow the road markers along the highway to get there. None of the sane people were on the road by that time. We arrived 6 -7 hours later, way past Fran's curfew at the dorm. Our guardian angels were working overtime on that trip.

Snow in Steamboat Springs and on Rabbit Ears Pass

Larry: Steamboat Springs was called Ski Town USA when we were growing up. We got a lot of snow in Mt. Harris and Craig but Steamboat got even more. In those days, the snow on the roads was just piled up along the sides and not hauled off as many places do today. I remember the snow being so deep along the main street that tunnels were dug out between the street and the stores. On Rabbit Ears Pass the highway department used large rotary snow "blowers" on trucks to literally cut their way through the snow. This produced a white wall of snow on either side 8 – 10 feet high sometimes so you couldn't see anything along the road. It was just like driving down the highway with a white wall on either side.

One time when I was coming back from college I was driving the red Ford up the east side of the pass. The road was winding and covered with snow. As I went around a corner the car lost traction, it didn't have much traction anyway, and spun around till I was heading up the road backwards on the wrong side of the road. Coming down the highway was a huge Cadillac. I had no control and was just waiting for the crunch as he ran into me. I don't know how, but he managed to go around me as I was careening toward him. My guardian angel must have nudged me out of the way. I ended up smashing into the snow wall along the road. That was wonderful! All I had to do was back away from the wall and continue up the highway.

Hunting and Fishing in Craig

Take your arms, your quiver, and bow, and go out: and when you have taken some thing by hunting, Make me savory meat thereof, as you know I like, and bring it, that I may eat: and my soul may bless thee before I die. **Genesis 27: 3-4**

Ed: Hunting and fishing were activities that we did every year. People from Minnesota, Wisconsin and Chicago would come to Uncle Antone's property to hunt. He had a large tent which would sleep around 10 people and that had a big stove in the middle. He used it as a camp tent for hunting parties. We only stayed there a couple of times because Dad really wasn't big on camping. He didn't think it was all that enjoyable but we would still go out hunting. It was fun for me.

The first time dad and I went hunting was when I had my own rifle, a 270. We went up on the rim rocks. From there we looked down onto a meadow and stayed for a couple of hours. It was dusk and since nothing had shown up, we headed back to the car. Dad said, "I think I see a couple of ears popping out of that bush up there." I looked up and said, "Where?" He whispered, "Right up there." "Oh, yeah." I had open sights and it was the first time I shot at anything. I raised the rifle and pulled the trigger. Dad was just amazed. "The deer disappeared. I guess you might have shot it." It was a four-point buck and I had shot it right through the neck. That was lucky because I didn't know what I was really aiming at. Dad wasn't very fond of deer meat but he brought it home and Mom cooked it.

Also, one time Dad and I were hunting on Papulous's land by Mt. Harris. We were up on another continuous ledge from which you could look down at a field. A herd of elk came out and they started running. Dad said, "Well, take a shot." So I was shooting. I think Dad actually shot one of them and it was a cow. We did not have a cow license so we had to go back to town. We got my cousins, Ralph and Tommy Knez, and the four of us went back there and quartered it. We had to carry it out and put it in the back of a pickup, cover it and stealthfully get it home so no game wardens would see us. That was a stressful night.

> We had to carry it out and put it in the back of a pickup, cover it and stealthfully get it home so no game wardens would see us.

We used to go fishing a lot, too. When we moved to Craig we would go up into the hills behind Uncle Antone's house. We drove Beaver Creek several times. It was still enjoyable because fishing was good and the area was so beautiful. I remember Uncle Antone, Dad, Delbert and I went up there and spent some time fishing. After a while we decided we didn't want to fish anymore. Delbert and I walked up the stream, got a couple of logs which we threw into the stream and then we jumped in and got on top of them. We rode them down the stream and, it was funny, when we came to the middle. Usually, you touched the bottom so you could keep yourself on the log upright, but we came to a really deep spot where I couldn't touch any more. I just rolled right over and Delbert saw me coming with my legs up out of the water still straddling the log, but with my feet straight up in the air. That was quite a ride! It is a wonder I didn't crack my head on something on the bottom of the stream. Those are the kinds of things we did just for cheap entertainment.

The other place we used to go fishing a lot was on Black Mountain where the fishing was excellent. There were also a lot of beaver dams in the gulches and valleys and a lake called Freeman Reservoir.

One time, Ken McClean and I cross country skied around Freeman Reservoir where there was a big building I had a key to. It was a good shelter so we went in to spend the night. There was a fireplace in the middle of a big open room and Tom Knez came up there on his snow mobile. He gathered a pile of wood and proceeded to build a fire in the fireplace. Unfortunately, the temperature just got colder and colder. We found out later it was 50 below zero that night. We put so many logs on the fire grate that it melted the grate to the floor. It just collapsed with the heat from the blazing fire we had going in the fireplace, but it still just barely kept us warm. We went outside during the night to see what it was like and the air was actually crystalizing. Not often do many people see this but it was so cold that the moisture in the air simply crystalized and shimmered in the light of the moon. The sight was unbelievably beautiful.

I have a couple of hunting stories I would like to tell. Dad told me that one time he and Uncle Antone were hunting up by the Fitzpatrick house which was quite a way from my Uncle's house. Of course, neither had a license to hunt. So they shot this buck, dressed it out and threw it in the back of the pickup. They were gone so long that Aunt Cleo and Mom were getting worried and were asking each other, "Where are Antone and Ralph?" And Aunt Cleo said, "Well, they have been gone a long time so we had better go see where they are."

They knew approximately where the men had planned to go so they got in the pickup and drove to where they thought the men were. Uncle Antone was about ready to get into their pickup and start it up when they saw lights coming. He and Dad jumped out of the pickup and hid along the road. It was little more than a path, just a mountain road. And then the lights would go away and they would jump into the pickup again and as soon as they were just about to start going they would see the lights come back around. They would jump out of the truck once more.

Well, the lights they were seeing were Aunt Cleo and my Mom looking for them, but of course, they didn't know that. They thought it could be a game warden so every time they saw the lights they would jump and hide and when the lights would go away they would get back in the truck. They eventually found out it was Mom and Aunt Cleo looking for them.

Another time, we were with Ralph and Helen Knez and I don't know why we were going up in the back country, but we were seeing something, checking something out or whatever. Driving up this mountain road we got to a spot where it was really wet and muddy and we had to get up the hill. Helen said to Ralph, "You can't make it up that hill. Don't even try it. We should just turn around and go back." Of course, my cousin, the Knez in him said, "No. I can make it." So he started up this hill again in four wheel drive and the wheels just sank into the mud. So we had to get out of the pickup. It was pretty late, actually it was after dark. We had to walk miles out of there. I think we walked to the Fitzpatrick house and it was 2-3 miles back. That was a difficult night.

Our family went fishing on our way back from Baggs, Wyoming. We drove over this bridge and stopped to check out the river. I can't remember if Mom and Dad were there but I know Larry and I were and we looked down into the water and we saw fish. One of them was huge. So we dropped our lines down and, of course, my brother with his luck got that fish. I think it was two pounds after it was dressed. It was the only fish that I saw my Mom bake and fill with stuffing. It was so, so good!

My cousin, Bobby, and I decided to go hunting. We climbed up to the top of a hill and looked down onto a field and saw some deer run out into the field. So we just unloaded! We were shooting, shooting, shooting as fast as we could! All of a sudden I looked up and there was a little clump of trees in the middle of the field and out of these trees came some men running for their lives because we were shooting down at the deer that were dashing up the field. What a situation! They were literally running for their lives along with the deer and we were shooting at these deer. That was an exciting experience. I'm glad we didn't hit one of the guys. That would have been a tragedy.

Working in Town

You may think it was a very little thing, and in these days it seems to me like a trifle, but it was a most important incident in my life. I could scarcely credit that I, the poor boy, had earned a dollar in less than a day. That by honest work, I had earned a dollar. I was a more hopeful and thoughtful boy from that time. **Abraham Lincoln**

Mowing lawns

Larry: I was in high school and I needed a job. Dad thought that mowing lawns might be something I could do so he bought me a lawn mower and I got a couple of customers. Before long I was getting more and more business and as soon as Ed was old enough he joined me in the work. We owned four 3.5 – 4 hp push lawn mowers and were mowing eighty lawns a week. We were pretty much the only game in town by that time.

Ed with Lawn Mowers

Dad would sharpen a stack of blades every day so the grass was cut perfectly. We changed the blades throughout the day. Work started as soon as the dew was off the grass and we always planned to finish before the afternoon showers at 3 pm. Each customer's lawn was mowed every week so we arrived at the homes on the same day and nearly the same time each week.

My first vehicle was an old 49 Buick. It wasn't in the best of condition and it shimmied violently at speeds over 40 mph. It was useful and got me to school periodically even though the high school was only two blocks away. I also used it for carrying our lawn mowers.

Ed and Larry with Lawn Mowers on the back of the Buick

When I left for Regis College in Denver, this was not suitable. I really wanted a 57 Chevy that was on the car lot at Watson Motors where Dad worked. The car was actually in great demand at the time so it was a bit pricey. Dad recommended a 54 Buick Roadmaster they had. The price was much lower but I argued that the Chevy would get better mileage. He just told me you would have to save a lot on gas to make up the difference.

The Buick was in good shape and quite fancy. It was huge, almost like a limousine and had a retractable antenna, a seek button on the radio and leg room to stretch out in the back seat. The baby blue paint job was oxidizing badly so I sanded the whole thing down and had it painted a beautiful metallic light blue. We had a metal lawn mower rack made that clamped onto the lip of the trunk with the lid open.

The lawn mowing business was doing really well so in a couple of years Ed bought a 1958 Ford pickup for the business. Of course, I would need a car for going to college so Dad found a 62 Ford Galaxy 500 hardtop to take to school. It had a black top and the lower body was a kind of metallic tan paint that had deteriorated quite a lot. I had that painted a cherry red and it was beautiful. It had a 4-barrel carburetor, a 390 cu in engine with a four speed transmission and overdrive. Nice.

Dad Mowing the Grass

Ed: When I was 10 years old my brother wanted to go into this business of lawn mowing and yard work. My Dad said, "Eddie, you're going to help your brother with this deal." I was thinking, "Really?" He said, "Yep, it's time you start working." I was only 10 years old! The first house that I worked at was Mrs. Stanton's, I believe. She had hired Larry to dig up dandelions in her yard. And that

> Dad said, "Yep, it's time you start working." I was only 10 years old!

became my job. My brother sent me over there and when I looked out over the yard I saw that there were thousands! She didn't just want them dug out, she had this thing called a *Killer Kane* that had a little squirter on the bottom of it. After digging up the dandelion you would take this *Killer Kane* and squirt poison into the hole down to the roots. I don't know how many dandelions I dug out in that yard but it was really thousands of dandelions. You had to use the *Killer Kane* to do it permanently. *(Larry: As I recall, we both worked on this project because one of us would dig and one would squirt. Maybe we traded off from time to time. We wore out a couple of Killer Kanes in the process. I remember going to Dad about half way through and saying we wanted to quit. We were sick of it. He told me, "You agreed to do the work and now you are going to finish the job." We finished and the dandelions didn't come back, and we cut Mrs. Stanton's lawn till we quit mowing.)*

We went more into a lawn mowing business from there and at one point we were mowing most of the lawns in town were hired out. And we really had it down pat. We would do a street on a certain day and we would handle 8-10 lawns on that street and then we would just go to the next street and do the same thing. We were very efficient at mowing lawns. We would take from 15 minutes to 30 minutes to mow a lawn depending on the size. The smallest lawn took us about 10 minutes.

Barbara, Eddie, Marlene, Dad, Larry Mom
1959

I remember one time I was pulling the lawn mower back up this hill and I slipped on a pile of dog manure and fell right in it. The side of my pants was all covered with dog manure and, of course, I just had to get out of those pants because they smelled so bad. I was gagging and I went to get into the pickup when Larry said, "Uh, you're not sitting up here." So I got in the back of the pickup instead.

The pickup was a blue 1958 Ford. I don't know who found the pickup, but probably my Dad did at the Ford garage. I had money in the bank so I could buy the pickup. So my Dad said, "You are going to buy this pickup for you and your brother's business." I said," I can't even drive." I was only 14 or 15 at the time. Dad said, "It doesn't matter you are going to buy it." And so, I bought the pickup and it was a year or so before I could drive it. It worked really well. Before that, my brother had this old Buick and he made this metal rack on the back of it to set the lawn mowers on. It was attached to the lip of the trunk and the bumper and it carried two lawn mowers. That's how we got around town from area to area to mow those lawns.

The mower engines would only last two years because the first year we would wear them out then we would bore the cylinder, put new rings in, recondition the engine and rebuild the carburetor so it would last another year.

Working for Empire Energy

Ed: I worked at the Empire Energy Coal Mine down in the canyon on the road south of town. It used to be the old Silengo mine. There are a couple of stories from then that are kind of funny, in a strange kind of way. I worked at the tipple where the coal trucks would come in and dump their coal. The coal would then go up on conveyors and be crushed. Afterward it would be loaded into the rail cars. Maxie Ciani was a repair man who worked for the mine. One day he came to do a job and we had to shut down the conveyor belt for him. He had to walk up the conveyer, I believe, to weld something that was broken. So while he was up there at the top I thought it would

> It started up and was sending everything to the crusher including Maxie Ciani.

be funny if I turned the conveyor belt on. It started up and was sending everything to the crusher including Maxie Ciani. He was on the conveyor that I knew I was going to turn off, but what a stupid idea! What if something went wrong and put him through that crusher? So I turned it off and he came flying off the machinery toward me. I had to lock the control cabin I was

in. This cabin was heated and it was there because when it got really cold in the winter you could still see what you were doing from the window. If I hadn't gotten in the cabin in time to lock the door he would have beaten the tar out of me. Fortunately, we later patched things up between us.

I also worked with Lenny Beck who was older than I was. I was in my early twenties and he was in his fifties. I would take a cable and attach it to the last coal car on the tracks and an electric motor would pull the cars by as we filled them. Well, Lenny released that motor so that it wasn't pulling any more. He didn't just stop it, he released it so it was like releasing the clutch in a car and when that occurred, suddenly all of the coal cars started rolling because they were on a slope on the track. The coal cars began accelerating and once that happened, there was nothing that was going to stop them. If he engaged the motor, it would just destroy it. There was a wheel on the cars that you turned to set the brake and I was jumping onto the coal cars to try to set it. Then, Lenny shouted, "Get off of there!!" He hollered at me because he saw that there was going to be a huge crash. Those coal cars had so much momentum it was unbelievable. They went right through the barricade at the end and almost up onto the road that was right next to the tipple. That was a nearly heart-stopping experience! Later, the coal company had to bring in a crane to lift the coal cars back onto the track.

> He hollered at me because he saw that it was going to be a huge crash.

Life after High School

College – Larry

There was never a time that I didn't think I would be going to college. Both Barbara and Marlene went to Loretto Heights College in Denver, a Catholic women's school run by the Sisters of Loretto. The obvious place for me to go then was to Regis College in Denver, a Jesuit college. I received a grant and a scholarship to go there, as I recall, and with what I earned mowing lawns it pretty much covered everything. It was a small school and had a nice compact campus.

Freshmen were hazed but it really wasn't anything over the top. We all had to wear brown and gold beanies with a propeller on the top. I had to polish the shoes of some seniors once. We

Regis College, Denver

were forbidden to wear white socks on the campus. One time a freshman was caught with white socks in the cafeteria and the seniors made him hang them from his ears and hop around the cafeteria shouting, "I am the Easter Bunny. I am the Easter Bunny."

The freshmen also had their own dormitory. It had very strict rules that were enforced by upperclassmen "prefects." They were responsible for ensuring order in the dorm. If you were playing a stereo too loudly, your prefect would just come in, unplug the device and confiscate it until he saw fit to return it. We weren't allowed to trash the place either or we would get written up. Freshmen were also expected to be at their desks from seven to nine in the evening and that was enforced as well. We were given a break between nine and ten and then had to be back at our desks again or in the sack. Ken Fehringer, from Peetz Colorado, was my roommate and we, along with anyone else who was interested, would frequently go to the nearby K-Mart and browse or buy a snack.

Edward and Larry

There was just enough room for the desk, bed and small closet/dresser with an aisle way in between. At lunch time guys would get together in our room (maybe they gathered in our room because we kept it orderly and clean, down to the waxed floor) to play the hearts card game. We set up the ironing board as a card table between two chairs in the aisle way and sat on the beds. That's how little space we had.

Playing Hearts in the Dorm Room

Except for a couple of dances where young women from Loretto Heights were bussed in, I don't remember a lot of entertainment on campus. We did all gather, however, each week to watch "*Batman*" on TV in the student center. We laughed and howled at the ridiculous dialogue and slapstick comedy. Every POW and BAM was echoed by the audience with gusto.

I came to Regis with the expectation that I was going to be an accountant. Dad was a bookkeeper/accountant and he seemed to enjoy it well enough. My accounting classes were taught by a Jesuit brother or seminarian. I don't know which because both wore cassocks and collars and when you are young it doesn't seem to be important. I did well in it but with considerable effort. By the end of the year, I decided that I couldn't imagine doing this for the rest of my life.

Fr. Murphy taught economics. That was an interesting class and something that was instructive even later in life as I now watch how economies work. Fr. McGinnis was the professor for my theology classes. He was a stern fellow and a hard taskmaster. There were quizzes nearly every day. We studied two things in that year; *The Idea of a University* by Blessed John Henry Newman and *The Documents of Vatican II*. I really should have been an expert on Vatican II after that class.

Larry Studying

I don't remember which priest taught literature but God bless him. (How was he able to do it year after year and remain sane?) The whole class was a study of James Joyce's *Portrait of the Artist as a Young Man*. We learned, or attempted to learn, every symbolic detail of every sentence at every level of understanding. The class is only memorable because I disliked it so much.

For fun I decided to join the college choir. It was fine except the director needed tenors so he decided I was going to be a tenor. I don't know what made him think that I might be able to sing that part. He even gave me a few lessons to develop the tenor in me but the strain nearly killed me and the resulting sound was more like a chicken squawking. That venture didn't last very long.

When I was attending Regis College I didn't have much spending money and neither did my friends. The Coors brewery was just up the road from the college in Golden, Colorado. It was less than fifteen minutes away so it was a perfect outing for young college guys. We would all get in a car and head to Golden for the free tour and a free beer at the end of the tour. No matter how many times we took the tour it was always interesting and enjoyable.

By the end of the year Ken Fehringer had decided he would continue his accounting degree at Colorado State University. I was ready to move on as well but not in accounting. I found out I could get a degree in commercial art at CSU so we both left for Ft. Collins the next fall.

Ken managed to find us an apartment in Ft. Collins just across College Avenue from the Old Main on the University. In the same apartment building were a couple of guys majoring in agriculture. They were just our type, or at least Ken's kind, as he and the other two came from farm/ranch country. Actually, we got along so well that we moved into a house together the next year.

Larry, Harvey Sprock, Gordon Valier and Snowman

I had taken most of my mandatory classes at Regis so almost all the rest of my classes were in art. That was fine with me, but I still had to take world history in a lecture class of about a hundred students. I also took psychology, logic, philosophy, and comparative religions. Between my year of theology at Regis and the philosophy classes at CSU I was just short of a philosophy minor. The psychology class was just something I had to wade through but I actually enjoyed the philosophy classes.

It wasn't long before I took figure drawing classes and discovered that the models were actually naked. After the initial shock, I was too busy churning out sketches to pay much attention to that astounding fact. In the drawing class we had to create one sketch after another on tablets of newsprint. We would draw and after a brief amount of time we had to tear it off and start another. Whew! We just threw those spontaneous sketches away.

> **Well it wasn't long before I took figure drawing classes and discovered that the models were actually naked.**

Art was making things, though, and I loved it. In sculpture we carved things, made molds for plaster, fiber glass and concrete figures. We started most of what we did in clay. I remember I was making a clay figure for a bust with a live model. I thought I was doing a great job when the instructor came up and said I had made a horse face and he took a spatula and cut off about half of the face and told me to start over. One thing about the instructor that people at the university today would find remarkable or even crazy was that he always wore a tie and a white smock.

My graphic art professors, Mr. Risbeck and Mr. Sorbie, were like that, too. They always wore a long sleeved shirt and tie, and most times a jacket. They were hard taskmasters! The assignments had to be on time, creative and executed meticulously. For every assignment each work was set up in front of the class for evaluation. More than once, one of the women in the class was reduced to tears by their critique.

> Heaven help any art education major that thought taking a commercial art course might be a fun thing to do.

I supposed some of the guys felt like it, too, but just didn't show it. Heaven help any art education major who thought taking a commercial art course might be a fun thing to do. They discovered very quickly that it wasn't what you would call "fun."

We were always making things in art classes whether it was oil painting, silk screen printing, ceramics or jewelry. In ceramics we got to create a work and then fire it in these super furnaces. In jewelry we were able to design and fashion pieces in gold and silver. A lot of it entailed cutting, hammering and soldering sheet silver but the best part was forming a piece in wax, making a mold and then melting the metal and forcing the molten metal into the mold with a centrifugal casting machine. That was not only fascinating, it was fun. One pendant I made was a combination of gold and silver and was quite an accomplishment to mold them together. I entered the pendant in an art contest on campus and won a $1000 scholarship. That was big money.

Ken and I are both Catholics so we spent time at the Newman Center not far off campus. At the beginning of our junior year we were at the Newman Center along with some freshman girls at an open house event. There were a couple of girls that caught our eyes. One was Fran Gastellum and Nancy someone. I don't know why but I offered Nancy a ride back to the dorm instead of the cute Italian girl. (I found out later that she wasn't Italian but Hispanic. No matter. I was smitten.) It wasn't even my car. It was Ken's. Well, actions have their consequences. I called Fran to ask her out on a date and said, "Hi, this is Larry Rutherford." An exasperated response was, "Larry, who!?" I humbly explained where we met and then she seemed to recall and agreed to go out with me.

I took Fran home for Thanksgiving the fall we met to introduce her to my family. After Thanksgiving dinner, Mom and Fran were cleaning up the kitchen. Mom picked up the turkey carcass and walked over to the garbage with it. Fran gasped and said "Aren't you going to make soup with that?" Mom said "No, I don't do that. Do you know how to make it?" Fran was embarrassed but thought she remembered how she had seen her mother do it, so she said, "I think so." So she put the carcass into a big pot, added water and celery as she had seen her mother do, and then she threw in a cup of rice. That didn't look like enough, so she threw in another cup. Before long, she had a gluey mess of rice in the pot, all stuck to the bones of the turkey!

Except for baking cookies, she had never really cooked at home. Being the fourth child, her job was to set the table and make the salad. Her sisters and mother did the cooking and she only saw parts of what they did. Little did she know that the carcass has to be cooked for several hours to extract the flavorful broth and then it has to be cleaned of all the meat. Afterward, the broth is strained and left to cool so the fat can be skimmed off, and only then, is it put back into the pot with rice and vegetables. Needless to say, she was most embarrassed as she had to carry the turkey with all the rice to the trash!

Fran came to CSU in September of 1967 at the ripe old age of 17 and lived in Allison Hall. Living in a women's dormitory, I emphasize Women's dormitory, is completely different that it is today. Girls today would liken it more to a nunnery if they were being nice. Each women's dorm had a dorm mother who was responsible to account for all the girls there. There was a curfew of 10 pm during the week and 12 pm on the weekends. Residents were required to sign out in the evenings and then sign in when they returned. The dorm mother stayed up until all the girls were accounted for. The next year, the girls were given card keys so there wasn't the same oversight as before. Whatever criticisms modern women might have of the system today, the young women had their privacy and were safe.

> The dorm mother stayed up until all the girls were accounted for.

Men were allowed in the dorm lobby but not in the resident's rooms except between 1 and 3 pm on Sundays. Even then the dorm room door had to be left open. The hall monitor, aka the resident assistant or RA, would walk up and down the halls to make sure everybody was behaving. Men were allowed in the public area of the dorm but no "pdas" (public displays of affection) were allowed in the building.

Once a month on a Sunday the dorm cafeteria was open to guests and the staff put on a fancy dinner. Sometimes steaks were served, other times ham with all the trimmings or other special dishes were prepared. It was always a nice occasion with tablecloths and tasty desserts. Fran usually invited me.

Fran and Larry going out

Everyone dressed up and it was a very enjoyable night out.

When Fran and I were engaged in October of her second year, she didn't tell anybody in the dorm until the occasion of her candle-passing. She informed the dorm mother who arranged for the ceremony. Since the floor monitor had been notified and passed on the word to the other residents on the floor, everybody came down dressed up for dinner. At this time, a number of tables had been set up in a rectangle for all the girls on Fran's floor. They were set with table cloths and

> The candle kept going around the table till it arrived at Fran who blew it out.

a special meal was served. At the appointed time, the dorm mother lit a candle and passed it to the girl at her right. The candle kept going till it arrived at Fran who blew it out. That was a special way for the news to be told in her dorm and Fran attended several such ceremonies during her two years living in Allison Hall.

When Fran arrived back in Colorado for her second year at CSU, the dorm situation had changed a lot. Everybody was given a key card to the front door and there was no longer a curfew. People took advantage of the situation and would leave side doors propped open for their friends to enter. It became harder to keep the guys out and it was the first step in the relaxation of dorm rules. It wasn't much longer before the idea of a dorm mother would be obsolete.

We spent a lot of time at the Newman Center for activities and outings. Father Leonard Urban was the chaplain; charismatic, eloquent, intelligent and gifted in many ways. He had the remarkable ability to remember names. He would go around the room of thirty people and once he heard their names he knew them. He had a special fondness for Teilhard de Chardin but I don't think any of the students thought there was any significance to that.

Fran and I played the guitars for Mass although we have repented for that many times in our more adult years. Some of the fine tunes we strummed and sang were "They'll Know We are Christians by our Love," "Sons of God," "Kumbaya," and "Let it be." What did we know? Songs seemed to cross the line seamlessly between camp fire and church. In any case, folk songs were what we enjoyed playing and singing the most so it all seemed fine for us.

> Songs seemed to cross the line seamlessly between camp fire and church.

We also went up into the mountains for field Masses. Things were quite casual then. All we needed was a folding table and a meadow surrounded by pine trees and mountains. That was our cathedral. Guitars seemed particularly suitable for the venue so it was all perfect.

Quest was the movement of the day for us young Newman Catholics. They were weekend retreats in the mountains at Camp St. Malo near Estes Park Colorado. It really couldn't be a better place to spend time, up in the fresh air surrounded by magnificent peaks and forests. Students were segregated by sex in open bay dormitories there. I am sure there were very inspiring talks and prayer but I don't remember any of it. I do remember that we made donuts by cutting the biscuit dough that comes in tubes into donut shapes, deep frying them and then sprinkling them with cinnamon sugar. Those were so good.

I also was impressed by the *Quest* challenge. Novices to the weekend were told that one of the things done at the *Quest* was to hike up Mt. Meeker, which loomed high above the camp, in the middle of the night and toboggan down the snow in the cleft on the face of the mountain.

> **Novices were told to hike up Mt. Meeker in the middle of the night and toboggan down the face of the mountain.**

They were convinced it was going to happen even until the time when everyone was ready to walk out the door and start the climb. The leaders explained that it was a test of trust, but that explanation didn't make sense to me. Would you trust anyone who would suggest going with them on a venture that would likely kill you?

Even though there was a lot of Vietnam War turmoil on many campuses around the country, the Aggies at CSU were quite conservative and largely kept out of the fray. The biggest controversy was when the students were demanding that beer be sold in the student center café. Ken, Fran, other reactionaries and I fought it with petitions and such. We believed that there were sufficient sources of beer around the town and campus already: Some so close that a thirsty student could walk over to a beer joint and stumble back without coming to a great deal of harm. We lost, of course. Why should the university let that source of revenue walk off the campus? Besides, it made the students happy. Win, win for them.

At the time of graduation, the Vietnam War was still going strong. Upon leaving college I would lose my II-S student deferment from the draft and would be reclassified I-A or available for service. The options were limited: Be drafted into the army and serve two years or join one of the other branches of the service and spend four years on active duty. Since I had my bachelor's degree I was eligible for the officer's corps, whichever I chose. I always liked tales of the sea and admired sailors so I took the naval officer's qualifying test. I didn't fail it but there were a flood of applications and I didn't make the cut.

Then I decided to take the Air Force Officer's Qualifying Test and passed. I had to wait for the results and get an Officer's Training School date so the recruiter advised me to enlist to be sure I got into the Air Force. As an airman I was selected to get a graphic arts specialty code. He put me into the delayed enlistment program and assured me that I would get an OTS date before I was actually inducted.

In the meantime, I got a great temporary summer job with the National Park Service in Rocky Mountain National Park. I was assigned to the trail crews. Each day we would leave our barracks with our tools, mattock and shovel, and hike up into the mountains. Our job was to repair trails, dig water diversion ditches and clear fallen timber. It was hard work but it was great to hike the trails in the park every day. We became so physically fit that we would race each other up the trails to the work sites.

One time we were working so far away from park headquarters that we had to stay in a cabin up in the mountains. That was a treat. The cabin was situated just next to a lake so we decided we would go swimming in it. There were five of us and each of us in turn jumped in and we barely hit the water before we scrambled out because it was icy cold. One guy, however, had a little more insulation than the rest of us and swam across and back. That really wasn't the smartest thing to do because there was no one who would have been able to help him if he got into trouble out in the middle.

Fran was working as a church volunteer with the migrant workers near Fort Lupton. She stayed in Greeley and would assist with taking people to the doctor and go on home visits to assess needs there. Since she spoke Spanish she was very helpful as a translator. She also played the guitar and sang at Masses out in the fields for the workers. We were already engaged by this time so on Sundays I would drive an hour and a half to Greeley and join her for Mass in the cucumber fields. What one does for love!

Military – Larry

In August I got my notification that I had to report to the Military Entrance Processing Station in Denver on September 2, 1969. I had to terminate my employment with the park service, get my things together and go to Denver. I arrived a day early and Marlene and Ralph let me stay at their home in Boulder with them. Since we had some time the day before, we went swimming at the local pool. It was probably the wrong thing to do. I got blisters from the sunburn down my back and on the tops of my feet. It was difficult sleeping for the first couple of nights in boot camp but it was worse marching in combat boots that hadn't been broken in. Since I was limping and having difficulties in marching I was sent to sick call to have them treated.

When we arrived at boot camp we were hustled down the clothing issue line and were fitted, more or less, with new uniforms. Then we were taken to our World War II barracks, shown how to put all our issued goods <u>neatly</u> and <u>precisely</u> into a footlocker at the end of our bunks. Exactly like in "No Time for Sergeants." We were instructed to write a post card to Mom and let her know we all arrived safely and convince her we weren't being mistreated. In the morning, we were awakened in what seemed to be the middle of the night to the sound of whistles and lights suddenly turned on. I was bewildered briefly – where was I anyway? -- but had to get moving and fall out in formation outside. We lined up in formation in Khaki pants, yellow T-shirts and pith helmets. We were a motley crew. It was September in Texas and it was soon blazing hot. At the entrance of every building were salt tablet dispensers to help prevent dehydration and sun stroke.

It wasn't long before we were all required to take a battery of immunizations. The Air Force was very efficient. We were lined up outside the clinic on the lawn and walked down a gauntlet where medics administered serum from a high pressure gun that literally squirted the serum into your arm. They just pressed this gun against your shoulder and the serum shot in a stream into your body. A lot of guys just fell over and passed out after it was over. Good thing the medics were already there.

> We walked down a gauntlet where medics administered serum from a high pressure gun that literally squirted the serum into your arm.

Halfway through boot camp I got a letter informing me that I had a class date for OTS for October. I had originally been selected for navigator training but now I was going into pilot training instead. I still was required to finish enlisted basic training in any case. I was thankful that I had my class date but that disrupted our plans for being married in November. All the arrangements for the wedding had to be changed to January and the invitations which had already been printed had to include a card saying that due to military commitments the new wedding date was 24 January 1970.

I went into OTS after a couple of weeks in casual control where I worked in the personnel office. OTS seemed quite a bit more difficult than basic training for me. There seemed to be more personal scrutiny and the academics were much harder. One interesting thing that was different was that we marched more in our tan 1505 uniforms with dress shoes than in the utility uniform. These shoes all had taps placed on the toes and heels of the shoes so when we marched it sounded very impressive.

Just like in basic training, we did a lot of marching. We marched everywhere, to classes, to barracks, to the mess hall. We frequently practiced marching as a squadron on the parade ground. All of us got the privilege of leading the formation as the squadron commander. Well, I never was known to have a good memory or have a quick wit, and I never liked being up in front of everyone. It was my turn to lead the squadron formation around the parade ground. Unfortunately, I forgot the necessary command and the timing to make a turn so I marched the entire squadron off the parade ground.

> Unfortunately, I forgot the necessary command and the timing to make a turn so I marched the entire squadron off the parade ground.

I did remember to give an inappropriate "squadron halt" that kept us on the air base, but my humiliation was almost complete. Lt. Walnum, the active duty squadron commander called me into his office to inquire about the debacle. Somehow I was able to talk my way out of the situation. Needless to say, I was not a distinguished graduate.

In my mind, however, graduation was my key to success and I was just happy to leave San Antonio.

At the same time, I was making plans to get married the day after graduation. The day after graduation! What kind of a plan was that?! I also was required to get a blood test before we were married so I had it done at Lackland AFB. I mailed it to Fran in Virginia and they discovered that Virginia would only accept a blood test done in the state. What a dilemma! That was impossible to get it done in time for the wedding. My father-in-law, thankfully, contacted his congressman there and he pulled strings to have my Air Force blood test accepted. In the meantime, our squadron was bussed into San Antonio for some time off and sightseeing. There wasn't a lot of time. I went shopping for a wedding gift for Fran and got her a pearl necklace. Then I called her from a telephone booth to visit for a couple of minutes. I laid the necklace in the box on the pay phone shelf and that's where I left it as the call ended. By the time I discovered my folly and got back to the phone, it was gone. So it was back to the jewelers for a second necklace.

2nd Lieutenant Rutherford

I finished up OTS in the top half of the class (how impressive), as I recall, but the greatest reward was getting the second lieutenant's "butter bars" and marching in the graduation parade. Immediately after our hats were thrown into the air, the "90 Day Wonder" was on a plane to Washington D. C. I don't quite know how I arranged the flight and everything considering how little free time we were given and everything had to be done by pay phone. In any case, it worked out and I got to the Gastellum home the same day. It was so wonderful to see Fran again.

Some dear friends of Louie and Aggie had a very lovely dinner planned for the evening at their home where both families and friends gathered to wish us well. The next day, the excitement began. Fran's father, in a fluster, was rushing some mints to the Charter House Hotel where the reception was to take place. In the process, he had a fender bender along the way.

So, the wedding was to take place at St. Michael's Parish in Annandale, Virginia. Msgr. Scannell, the pastor was skeptical of the priest who was going to officiate at the ceremony. Fr. Leonard Urban was the chaplain for the Newman Center at Colorado State University and we had asked him to perform the ceremony. Apparently, college chaplains had already gotten a reputation for being a bit unorthodox, so Msgr. Scannell warned us he would be monitoring the wedding from the rectory via the intercom and if our priest starts, "dancing on the altar" or something like that, and he would come to the church and stop the whole darn event. Everything was normal, thankfully, so we were married, had a lovely cake, finger foods and a champagne fountain afterward at the hotel.

> Msgr. Scannell warned us that if our priest starts "dancing on the altar" he would stop the whole darn event.

After the reception we went back to the Gastellum house to open presents. That being done and with goodbyes to family we left for my first assignment at Williams AFB in Arizona and our new life as a married couple.

Epilogue

Eulogy for Our Dad

Marlene: Our father, Ralph Charles Rutherford was born July 3, 1916, on his family's ranch near Hayden, Colorado. He was the second of seven children born to Charles and Daisy Rutherford. Born with a natural ear for music, Dad learned to play the mandolin and piano exceptionally well without formal music lessons. This was a talent won naturally through his mother's family as they were all musicians. Also every member of his family was so musically talented that a family band was formed that performed regularly at dances throughout the Yampa Valley for many years.

On June 10th, 1939, he married the love of his life, our mother Marie Knez in St. Michael's Church. He became a Catholic and fervently embraced the Faith. For 60 years of marriage he was a role model as a loving, caring, dedicated, and understanding husband. His exceptional love for Mom became even more evident towards the end of her life. He did everything possible to care for her at home and to maintain her human dignity as she was eventually taken from us by Alzheimer's disease.

Dad and Mom participated fully in this vocation and lovingly raised four children: Barbara, Marlene, Lawrence, and Edward. To Dad and Mom, children were a special blessings and responsibility from God. By their example and guidance, we were taught the power of prayer in our lives, especially through weekly Mass, the Eucharist, and the daily recitation of the rosary. Dad and Mom nurtured us spiritually, mentally, and physically. We were a close family that prayed, worked and played together.

Dad enjoyed getting together with family and friends and had a good time regardless what the occasion was. He particularly enjoyed having dinner parties at his home and continued to do so after Mom's death. When can we not think of Dad and remember his sense of humor? He was an optimist who was able to see the good or humorous side in every situation. Many times he laughed so hard that tears ran down his cheeks.

One of his most relaxing and enjoyable activities was playing golf which he did on a regular basis for many years. As he got older and his eyesight became weaker, people were amazed that he could still hit the ball.

Dad was an honest, hard-working man who taught us the importance of working and doing our best at whatever we undertook. It was clearly understood that we were expected to act responsibly and follow through with our commitments. Children were always very special to Dad and he enjoyed playing and, on a rare occasion, teasing them a bit. Not surprisingly, he was an avid pro-life supporter.

Due to Dad's failing health and weight loss, he was brought to Ft. Collins in March 2005 and was diagnosed with terminal cancer. He did not complain or feel sorry for himself and instead was joyful and grateful to everyone who visited him or assisted him in any way. He continued to be a role model to the very end with his patience, love, faith, and acceptance of God's will. His was a life well lived and he is greatly missed by all.

Eulogy for Our Mom

Marlene: Our mother Marie Laura Knez Rutherford was born November 15th 1920 on her family's ranch south of Craig. Since her death at home last Sunday evening, I have had time to reflect on her life and I now liken it to a beautiful rainbow with each color representing a different facet of her life.

When I think of red, I am reminded of her tremendous love and devotion to our Lord, Jesus Christ and to His church. To our father Ralph Rutherford, her loving husband of 60 years and to her children, Barbara, Lawrence, Edward and me, Marlene. She was also very fond of and proud of her daughters in law, Fran and (before her death) Trish and sons in law Ken Martin and Ralph Henderson. She embraced the duties and responsibilities of her life as a wife and mother and together with our father, taught us the importance of prayer in our lives, in particular, to pray the rosary. Mom also taught us to love and respect all people and to always strive to develop good moral values. One of her greatest joys was getting all of us together for family gatherings that often included exquisite meals.

She loved people and derived great joy from welcoming new members of the community into her home and heart saying, "There's always room for one more at our table."

The color orange brings to mind her many talents and abilities. Exceptionally gifted as a seamstress, her family enjoyed an endless variety of beautiful clothing which she prepared with extraordinary pride and dedication for each member's daily life, as well as for special occasions. She was particularly proud of the many linens and banners she lovingly crafted for the church and enthusiastically and faithfully worked on numerous items for the church bazaar year in and year out.

The color yellow reminds me of the joy she felt for all children and especially for her grandchildren and great grandchildren. Her tremendous love for and joy in children was evident in her support of the crusade for the Right to Life. In the last few years of her life, the joy she felt for any baby or small child in her presence was particularly evident.

The color green is reminiscent of her green thumb. Her lifelong interest in gardening produced incredibly beautiful and varied plants and flowers. In this regard, she is perhaps best remembered for her back yard flower garden which incorporated the statue of the Virgin Mary as its dominant theme.

The color blue brings to mind the overwhelming concern she felt for all human beings. She could not fathom the atrocities occurring around the world that we were all aware of through daily news programs. She strove for perfection in an imperfect world and because of this, she carried far more than her share of burden throughout her life.

The color purple is representative of the sorrow of her last few years. Mom was aware that something was badly wrong. One day at the onset of her disease, Mom telephoned Aunt Louise and tearfully told her she no longer remembered how to make an apple pie. Aunt Louise lovingly went to her house and together the apple pie was made. Shortly after, Mom was diagnosed with Alzheimer's.

We do not know when we marry what kind of crosses we will be called upon to bear, but our parents have always been very dedicated to one another. Through their Faith, they have continued to share a love and respect for each other that carried through to the end of her life.

Dad loved Mom more than words can express, and she loved him equally as much. She would say to us that we had an angel for a Daddy. Does anyone ever remember them addressing each other by their names? Ralph or Marie/Mickey? I can only remember lots of "Honeys" and "Sweethearts". Barbara

Changing Times

Ed: Our kids will never know the freedom that we had. Larry and I used to hunt rabbits together, fish, and hang out in the mountains. We just enjoyed things. It was a very free place to grow up. It was freedom with responsibility. Because you have to be responsible. Everybody watched each other's kids and when you were out of line there were consequences.

Larry: When we lived in Mt. Harris we were poor. We didn't know we were poor as we had sufficient clothing, food, a home and a car; pretty much like everyone else in the camp. But by today's standards, however, we were poor. We didn't have the gadgets, the electronics, "time saver" appliances like automatic washer, dryer and dishwasher, multiple cars, motor boats, RVs, ATVs, etc. etc. No fancy homes. We almost never went out to dinner (maybe occasionally to the A & W Root Beer stand), rare vacations, few clothes and toys.

We also didn't have computers and cell phones for communications. Mostly people talked to each other. We frequently dropped by friends' and families' homes for a cup of coffee and stayed late into the evening. We could do that because people were home and they opened the door to you. You actually knew your neighbor. Truly, you knew everyone in town. Pot luck get-togethers featured a plethora of the resident ladies' specialty dishes. Store-bought was unheard of. There were lots of community organizations and local sports to go to. Most of the sports heroes were in town. We had the outdoors to fish and hunt in; to have picnics and to hike in; to drive out into the countryside to look at the deer or elk; to play in a running stream in the forest. Maybe we were actually rich.

Kids could roam around the town and there was no fear from other people (unless you were doing something you shouldn't be doing. Then you were called to task and your parents heard about it.) Talking back to parents could merit the back of the hand. What parents might be concerned about when you were out were the river, the trains, the mine operations, the rattlesnakes, falling off cliffs, wood ticks and such.

There was a common sense of moral propriety. Those who lied, cheated, loafed, were unfaithful to their spouse were disdained. People were generally as good as their word. Weddings and marriages were celebrated as a lifelong adventure ... for better or for worse. There was no sense of entitlement.

People worked hard, not necessarily because they loved their work but because they had to earn a living or go hungry. They labored under hazardous and deadly conditions. Many who survived lived with chronic health conditions. There were hazards in life which everyone accepted as, well, life. Consequently, our lives were not governed by government directives and threats of litigation.

Conversely, it seems to me, what we have today is a spiritual poverty, a poverty of time, a poverty of community, a poverty of relationships, a poverty of true freedom, homes packed full of stuff in which there is a poverty in excess and, finally, a poverty of hope. Possibly this flows from a nihilistic culture and the heresy of utilitarianism. It makes one weep!

Barbara: If I compare my childhood with that of a youth of today, there are stark differences. Having been born at the beginning of the fourth decade of the twentieth century, I think the most glaring difference is the simplicity of life that we lived. There was stability and routine in our lives.

Divorce was unheard of. In our immediate family, there were no divorces until that of Uncle Leonard and Aunt Carol. Dad said that when there was a marriage, it was expected that it would last forever--or as stated in the marriage vows "until death do us part." I knew there were imperfect marriages in our family but I never ever thought that the marriage would end in divorce. There was an acceptance of suffering and perseverance that disappeared with the passage of time.

Dad worked at his job; Mom was at home with us children. Very few women were in the workplace in Mt. Harris. I think there may have been one or two who worked in the stores.

We had one car (no seat belts) that took us where we wanted to go on the weekends. The car was rarely used during the week. Dad walked to work and Marlene, Larry and I walked to school without a moment of fear. When it was time to go to high school, we had a regular routine of catching the bus uptown (or in the school play yard) and returning every day about 3:30 p.m.

There were few extracurricular activities other than basketball and football. Meetings of clubs took place during the school day. We had school and community dances where young people had a chance to meet others and connect.

We didn't have the distractions which came with TV or social media. We had a radio which Mom monitored very effectively. Elvis was not permitted as part of our listening repertoire. Most popular music of the 40's and 50's was easy to listen to as simple love songs. By the end of the 50's, the rock and roll became more agitating. We were heading toward the 60's which were very destructive, from my vantage point.

We talked to each other face to face and had dinner together as a family. The phone (when accessible) meant you could actually connect to another person and not to a fake recording.

We trusted other people and knew that most people were honest in their dealings with each other. Mom and Dad did lock our house with a skeleton key which really wasn't much security because it wasn't that necessary.

As I have said before, my growing up days were very happy days in my life. I am going to quote Peter Kreeft because he says well what I think about my young life.

"Nobody makes a TV show about kids today with a title like "Happy Days."

Appendices

Appendix 1 - Rutherford Family Tree

David Rutherford (1690) – Mother unknown

> David Rutherford left Fairington, Scotland and went to Jamaica about 1716

John Rutherford I (1720) – Elizabeth Elliot (1723)

John Rutherford II (1750) – Mother unknown
5 children

John (Jack) Rutherford III (1780) - Winnie Grigsby (1784)
Virginia – Hawkins Co.,TN
10 Children

> Family Sailed to North Carolina, USA in 1751

Bayless E. Rutherford (1815) – Mary Catherine Curtis (1835)
Prairie Grove Ark. – Prairie Grove Ark.
15 children

William Rutherford (1855) – Parthena Colyer (1857)
Fayetteville, Ark. – Indiana
10 children

Charles Clay (Coke) Rutherford (1894) – Daisy Squire (1896)
Tulsa, Okla. Indian Territory – Hayden, CO
7 children
Juanita (Camiletti), Ralph, Francis, Marie (Turner), Wanda (McDonald), Leonard, Loren

Ralph Rutherford (1916) – Marie Knez (1920)
4 children
Barbara (Martin), Marlene (Henderson)
Lawrence Rutherford, Edward Rutherford

Appendix 2 - Mahowald Family Tree

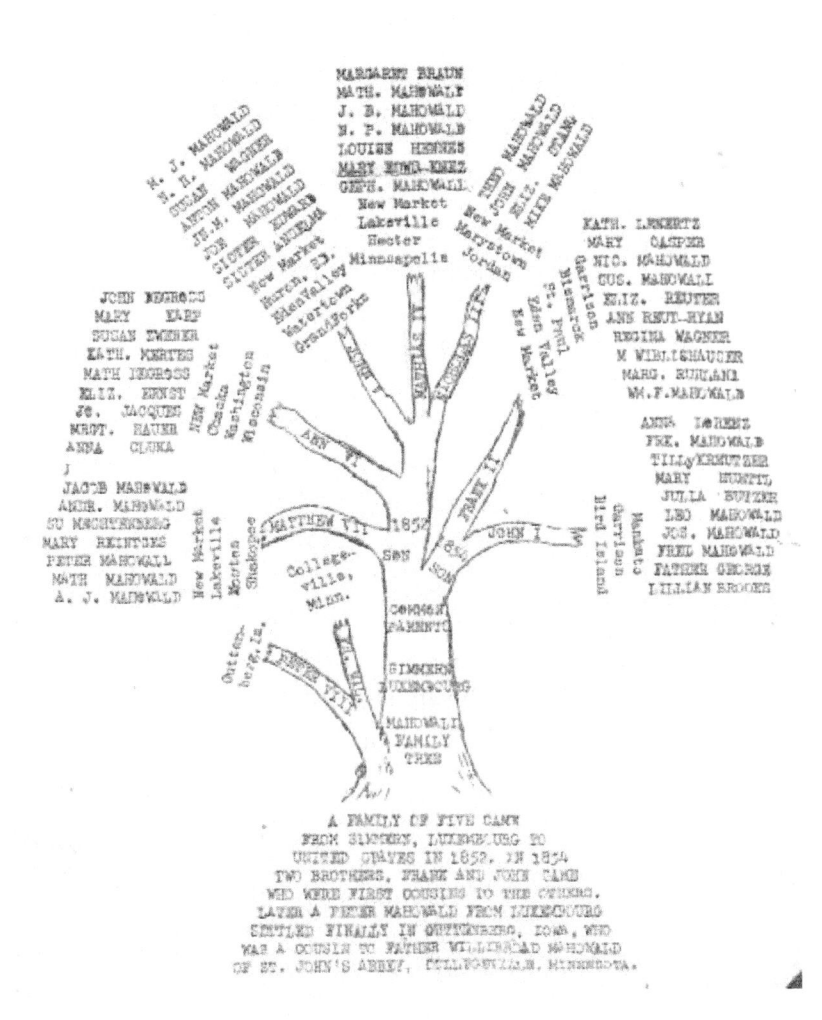

MARGARET BRAUN
MATH. MAHOWALD
J. B. MAHOWALD
N. P. MAHOWALD
LOUISE HENNES
MARY EDER-ENEZ
GEPH. MAHOWALD
New Market
Lakeville
Hector
Minneapolis

M. J. MAHOWALD
N. H. MAHOWALD
SUSAN WAGNER
ANTON MAHOWALD
JN.M. MAHOWALD
JOE. KOHLER
SISTER ANDREA
New Market
Hector, Sp.
Glen Valley
Watertown
Grand Forks

FRED MAHOWALD
LIZ. STAHR
MIKE MAHOWALD
Margystown
Jordan

KATH. LENERTZ
MARY CASPER
NIC. MAHOWALD
GUS. MAHOWALD
ELIZ. REUTER
ANS REUT-RYAN
REGINA WAGNER
M WIBLISHAUSER
MARG. RUHLAND
WM.F.MAHOWALD

Garrison
St. Paul
Glen Valley
New Market

JOHN NEGRESS
MARY KARP
SUSAN EWENER
KATH. MERTES
MATH NEGRESS
ELIZ. ERNST
JO. JACQUES
MRGT. RAUER
ANNA CLUKA
JACOB MAHOWALD
AMER. MAHOWALD
SU MECHTENBERG
MARY REINTGES
PETER MAHOWALD
NATH MAHOWALD
A. J. MAHOWALD

New Market
Omaha
Washington
Wisconsin

New Market
Lakeville
Morton
Shakopee

MATTHEW VII 1852
Collegeville, Minn.

FRANK VI 1854
Son

JOHN I
Son

ANNA LORENZ
FRK. MAHOWALD
TILLY KREUTZER
MARY HUMPTY
JULIA BUTZER
LEO MAHOWALD
JOS. MAHOWALD
FRED MAHOWALD
FATHER GEORGE
LILLIAN BROOKS

Manato
Garrison
Bird Island

COMMON
PARENTS

SIMMERN
LUXEMBOURG

MAHOWALD
FAMILY
TREE

PETER VIII
Ottenberg, Ia.

A FAMILY OF FIVE CAME
FROM SIMMERN, LUXEMBURG TO
UNITED STATES IN 1852. IN 1854
TWO BROTHERS, FRANK AND JOHN CAME
WHO WERE FIRST COUSINS TO THE OTHERS.
LATER A PETER MAHOWALD FROM LUXEMBOURG
SETTLED FINALLY IN OTTENBERG, IOWA, WHO
WAS A COUSIN TO FATHER WILLIBRAND MAHOWALD
OF ST. JOHN'S ABBEY, COLLEGEVILLE, MINNESOTA.

Appendix 3 - Squire Family Tree

**William (1814) and Mary Squire (1812)
Parents of Albert Squire**

|

**Albert Squire (Grandma's father) (1853
Mina L. Squire (mother) 1858)**

|

Mary Belle Squire (1881) died as a newborn
Sadie Maude (1882)
Minnie E. Squire (1883)
Margery E. Squire (1885)
Lena May Squire (1887)
Franklin A. Squire (1890)
Reuben Squire (1892)
Pearl Squire (1894)
Calvin Squire (1898)
Joe Squire (1900)
Andy R. Squire (1903)
**Daisy Squire (1896)
Charles Rutherford (1895)**
Juanita
Ralph
Frances
Marie
Wanda
Leonard
Loren

Mina Squire (Grandma's mother died in 1904 and her father married Martha M. Watts, stepmother, in 1905). There were no children born of this union

Appendix 4 Rutherford/Knez Cousins

Juanita and Alfred Camiletti Sonny (d) - Eugene Pat (d) Darrell Christie (d) **Ralph and Marie Rutherford** Barbara Marlene Larry Edward **Francis and Doris Rutherford** Linda Beverly **Marie and Bo Turner** Janice Frances Dee (d) Chuck (d) Randy (d) **Wanda and Fred McDonald** Ron Carol (d) Sherry Duane Danny	**Leonard and Carol Rutherford** Ann **Loren and Dorris Rutherford** Laura Christopher (d) Karen (d) Brenda (d?) **Roselyn Carter** Marie Richard (d) **Louise Charlie Fedinec** Edith Joy Leon (d) **Joseph and Virginia Knez** Veronica Linda David Paul Theresa Margaret Mary Ann (d) Joseph (Jody) Mike	**Raymond Grace/Helen Knez** Ramona Fred (d) Lewis Martin Madeleine Rosalyn Loretta Pete (d) Jaqueline Gregory **Antone and Cleo Knez** Thomas Ralph (d) Delores Robert (d) Delbert John (d)

Appendix 5 – Children, Grand Children and Great Grand Children

Barbara and Ken Martin
- *Kristin Martin*
- *Monica and Dan Oldenburg*
  - Clare Marie
  - Dominic William
  - Cecilia Rose
  - Gianna Elizabeth
  - Joseph Daniel
  - Brigid Irene
- *Brenda and John Firth*
  - Ethan John
  - Thomas William
  - Stephen Charles

Marlene and Ralph Henderson
- *Michelle and Craig Van Wagner*
  - Michelle Ashley Tuntland

- *Monique and Milton Duane Tudahl, Jr.*
  - Zoe Jade

- *Sean and Lisa Henderson*
  - Nicole

- *Todd and Beth Henderson*
  - Alexander Sean
  - Carmen Isabelle

Lawrence and Frances Rutherford
- *Ian and Paula Rutherford*
  - Lucy Erin Elizabeth
  - Margaret Mary
  - Andrew Caspian Nicholas
  - Anne Catherine Bernadette
  - Susan Monica Therese
  - Peter Julian Benedict
  - Maria Isabel Andrea
  - Thomas Edmund Paul
  - Robert James Kieran
  - Felicity Juliana Rose
  - Claire Josephine Marie

- *Erin Patricia* (d)

- *James and Breanne Rutherford*
  - Genevieve Helen
  - Bernadette Francesca
  - Madeleine Noelle

- *Rebekah and Moses Delgado*
  - Benedict Robert Harris
  - Isabella Faustina Harris
  - Phillip Michael Delgado

- *Michael Rutherford*

Edward and Patricia Rutherford
- *Sean Daniel and Julie Ann (Gill) Rutherford*
  - Jacob Daniel
  - Patrice Rose
  - Madelyn Grace
  - Caela Mae

- *Sarah and Christopher Lindgren*
  - Connor Michael
  - McKenzie Patricia
  - Dylan Edward
  - Aiden Jeffrey
  - Teagan Eileen

- *Ellen and Michael Doherty*
  - Emily Patricia
  - Ariana Marie
  - Addison Catherine
  - Jackson Patrick
  - Kolbe Edward

- *Caitlin and Cole Emerson*
  - Tavian Larkin James
  - Felicity Patricia Eileen
  - Beckett Edward James
  - Ephrem Colby James

- *Andrea and Luke Vercolone*
  - Augustine Patrick
  - Gemma Michaela
  - Estella Maris
  - Zaylee Louise

Appendix 6 – Photo Album

Grandpa Knez

Grandma Knez

Dad, Larry, Grandma Knez, Barbara and Marlene

Grandma Knez and a Friend

Grandma Knez, Barbara and Marlene

Grandpa and Grandma Knez and Family

Grandpa and Grandma at the Ranch

Aunt Louise on horse, Uncle Joseph, Grandpa, Uncle Antone, Fr. Brady, Mom and Grandma

Joseph, Mom, Antone, Louise and Raymond

Roselin Carter and Marie Carter

Roselin Carter

Marie Carter

Marie Carter

Roselin Carter First Communion

Mom and Dad

Mom's Graduation 1939

Mom and Dad at the Ranch

Dad on Rabbit Ears Pass

Mom with a Hula Hoop

Rutherford Kids

Barbara and Marlene

Barbara and Marlene

Eddie and Larry in front of Depot

Larry and Eddie

Uncles in the Military

Antone Knez

Francis Rutherford

Loren Rutherford

Leonard Rutherford

Appendix 7 – Dad's Letter to Mom

Mount Harris Colo.
January 5, 1939

Dearest Micky,

Well honey here I am again making a nuisance out of myself as always, but I am going to write anyway.

You know kid I intended to come down earlier the other night when I had to bring those kids down, but when I went home from work that night, my uncle was there and I had to play music until 8:00. I was almost afraid to come out it was so late, but I am glad I did now.

Darn I guess I won't get to see you again before Sunday, because I have to help at the dance Saturday night since our basketball team is giving it. I wish you could go but I don't believe your dad likes it when you go to the dances. I know he didn't like it the other day when you went skating, and I guess that was my fault. I guess we will just have to forget about skating and dances until you get well enough to do it. We can go to the show on Saturday nights, and maybe that wont bother you.

I haven't been doing much of anything this week but working. Monday night we played the Hayden High School Team and beat them 51 to 42. We have only lost one game so far, so I think we are doing pretty good.

You know honey it is sure going to seem funny not getting to see you Saturday night, but we will make up for it Sunday. We will do something during the day, then go to the show that night.

My letter writing is getting worse and worse. See I have run down again, and can't think of anything more to write except I will be down Sunday about 11:00.

Till then

Lots of Love
Ralph

Ralph Rutherford
Mount Harris, Colo.

Miss Marie King
Box 206
Craig, Colorado

Appendix 8 – Mom and Grandma Knez

Mom's Calendar Notes for March 1950

1 Wed - Washed clothes	**2 Thurs** - Gave Barbara a permanent wave	**3 Fri** - Gave Marlene a permanent, ironed and cleaned house	**4 Sat** - Mother and Virginia came up. In the evening, we went down to Cleo and Antone's
5 Sun - Went to Mass in Craig. Family was at Mother's for dinner.	**8 Wed** - Ida and kids had dinner with us.	**9 Thurs** - Washed and cleaned house. Margie, and Ralph's folks came to dinner.	**11 Sat** - Cleaned house. B. Merle came down tonight.
12 Sun Went to the show in Steamboat	**14 Tues** - Mom and Dad came up.	**16 Thurs** - Snowed	**18 Sat** - Leonard and Carol came. Dance at Craig. Stormed/snow.
19 Sun - Antone and Cleo and family came up for dinner. All of us were tired from the dance.	**20 Mon** - Ida served with me. Haskes came down in the evening. Made two dresses for Ann Rutherford.	**22 Wed** - Made four dresses † for me, Barb, Marlene and Lin Walker.	**23 Thur** Washed. Leonard and folks came down for supper.
24 Fri - Washed clothes. Made Marlene a coat.	**25 Sat** - Made Barbara a coat. Ralph's folks came down in the evening. Ida left James.	**26 Sun** - Mother was sick. Had a school board meeting and me and the kids went down to Haskes for a while then we went down home.	**27 Mon** - Stormed
28 Tues – Did a little sewing. Made a dress for me. (pink)	**29 Wed** – Washed. Made two aprons. (show)	**30 Thurs** - Ironed	**31 Fri** - Show

Barbara: Aunt Cleo, whose mother died when Aunt Cleo was ten, was subsequently hired as a teen by Grandma Knez to help on the farm. She became a good friend of Mom, Aunt Louise and Little Marie, fell in love with Uncle Antone and married him in the "forties." She was well aware of the work schedule on the farm and so related to me the events in Grandma's day. They are as follows:

1. Arise early to **cook breakfast** for family members and hired help (including miners)
2. Set up and **start the wash** by putting the clothes in the boiler on the stove.
3. **Make bread** and go to the fields to **plow a couple of furrows.**
4. Return to the house and **hang clothes.**
5. Finish the bread and **make lunch.**
6. Go back to the fields to **plow more furrows.**
7. Return to the house to **make supper.**
8. After eating, she sometimes **went to the coal mine** to help out.

Grandma Knez on the Ranch

Barbara: I have always said that Grandma was one of the most liberated women in the world because she could do the hard work of anyone- male or female. No pansy in her. Mom told the story about one of Grandma's experiences in Grandpa's mine. One of the miners was half-heartedly shoveling coal into the mine cart. When Grandma saw how little he was doing she told him to give her the shovel and she would show him how it was done. She then lifted double the amount of coal on the shovel and heaved it into the cart, shovel full after shovel full. The man watched in amazement.

Appendix 9 - Top Movies 1940 - 1970

Movies in the 1940's
1. **Casablanca (1942)**
Humphrey Bogart, Ingrid Bergman
2. **Citizen Kane (1941)**
Orson Wells
3. **It's a Wonderful Life (1946)**
Jimmy Stewart, Donna Reed
4. **The Maltese Falcon (1946)**
Humphrey Bogart, Mary Astor
5. **Bambi (1942)**
6. **Pinocchio (1940)**
7. **Fantasia (1940)**
8. **Arsenic and Old Lace (1944)**
Cary Grant, Pricilla Lane
9. **Rebecca (1940)**
Laurence Olivier, Joan Fontaine
10. **Shop Around the Corner (1940)**
Jimmy Stewart, Margaret Sullivan
11. **Twelve O'clock High**
Gregory Peck
12. **Jane Eyre (1943)**
Orson Wells, Joan Fontaine
13. **Miracle on 34th Street (1947)**
Edmond Gwenn, Maureen O'Hara

Movies of the 1950's
1. **The 10 Commandments (1956)**
Charlton Heston, Yul Brynner
2. **Shane (1953)**
Alan Ladd, Jean Arthur
3. **The Greatest Show on Earth (1952)**
Charlton Heston, James Stewart
4. **Rear Window (1954)**
James Stewart, Grace Kelly
5. **On the Waterfront (1954)**
Marlon Brando, Carl Malden, Rod Steiger
6. **High Noon (1952)**
Gary Cooper, Grace Kelly
7. **Around the world in 80 Days (1956)**
David Niven, Cantinflas
8. **The Bridge on the River Kwai (1957)**
Alec Guinness, William Holden
9. **Old Yeller (1957)**
Fess Parker, Dorothy McGuire
10. **Ben Hur (1959**
Charlton Heston, Jack Hawkins, Stephen Boyd

Movies of the 1960's
1. **The Manchurian Candidate (1962)**
Frank Sinatra, Angela Lansbury, Janet Leigh
2. **Lawrence of Arabia (1962)**
Peter O'Toole, Alec Guinness, Omar Sharif
3. **My Fair Lady (1964)**
Audrey Hepburn, Rex Harrison
4. **Sound of Music (1965)**
Julie Andrews, Christopher Plummer
5. **A Man for All Seasons (1966)**
Paul Scofield, Orson Welles, Vanessa Redgrave
6. **Oliver (1968)**
Mark Lester, Ron Moody, Shani Wallis
7. **To Kill a Mockingbird (1962)**
Robert Duvall, Gregory Peck
8. **Mary Poppins (1964)**
Julie Andrews, Dick Van Dyke
9. **The Great Escape (1963)**
Steve McQueen, Richard Attenborough, James Garner
10. **Dr. Zhivago (1965)**
Omar Sharif, Julie Christie, Alec Guinness
11. **Judgement at Nuremberg (1961)**
Judy Garland, William Shatner, Marlene Dietrich

Appendix 10 - Family Recipes

Pie Crust

Pie Crust (Mom)

4 c flour
1 T sugar
2 t salt
1 ¾ c. shortening
1 T vinegar
1 large egg

Put 1st 3 ingredients in bowl & mix with fork. Add shortening & mix till crumbly. In small bowl beat together with fork ½ c water, vinegar, & egg. Combine the 2 mixtures, stirring with fork, until all ingredients are moistened.

Best Rum Cake Ever   Antone Knez

1 or 2 quarts of rum   1 cup dried fruit
1 cup butter   1 teaspoon soda
1 teaspoon sugar   Lemon juice
Brown sugar   Nuts
Baking powder   2 large eggs

Before you start, sample the rum to check for quality (good, isn't it?) Now go ahead. Select the large mixing bowl, measuring cup, etc. Check the rum again. It must be just right. To be sure rum is of the highest quality, pour one level cup of rum into a glass and drink it as fast as you can. Repeat.
With an electric mixer, beat one cup of butter in a large fluffy bowl. Add one seaspoon on thugar and beat again. Meanwhile, make sure that the rum is of the finest quality. Try another cup. Open second quart if necessary. Add 2 large leggs, 2 cups fried druit and beat till high. If druit gets stuck in beaters, just pry it loose with a drewscriver. Sample the rum again, checking for tonscisticity.
Next, sift 3 cups peppar or salt (it really doesn't matter which). Sample the rum again. Sift 1/2 pint of lemon juice. Fold chipped butter and strained nuts. Add 1 babblespoon of brown thugar, or whatever color you can find. Mix mel. Grease oven and turn cake pan to 350 gredees. Now pour the whole mess into the coven and ake. Check the rum again and go to bed.

245

Dad's Pancake Recipe

1 cup Flour
1 cup buttermilk (fresh milk may be substituted. Add 1 tablespoon of vinegar to the milk and let stand for 5 minutes)
1 tbsp. sugar
1 tsp. baking powder
2 tbsp. cooking oil
½ tsp. salt
½ tsp. baking soda
1 egg (beat well)

Place all dry ingredients into a mixing bowl and whisk till combined. Add milk, cooking oil and egg and stir with whisk till all the lumps are gone.

The batter should pour from the dipper but not be too thin. If you use buttermilk, you may need to add a bit of milk to get the right consistency. Grease the griddle before each pancake so each one is nice and brown. Turn pancakes as soon as they are puffed up and full of bubbles, but before they break ... important for light cakes.

Caribbean Punch Bowl

Oatmeal Cookies

Mom's Oatmeal Cookies
- 1 C. Coconut
- 2 eggs
- 1 C. white sugar } 1st cream these together
- 1 C. brown sugar
- 1 C. lard
- 2 C. flour
- 2 t. baking powder
- 1 t. soda
- 3 T. hot water
- 4 C. oatmeal – don't use quite 4 c.

Bake at 375° for 10 min.

Poppy Seed Cake

Mom's Poppy Seed Cake

Soak ½ cup poppy seeds in 1 cup of milk for one hour. Cream ½ cup butter with 1 cup sugar + 1 t vanilla. Sift 3 cups flour with ½ t salt. 2 t. baking powder. Add to butter and sugar mix alternately with poppy seeds and milk. Fold in stiffly beaten egg whites of 4 eggs. Bake in greased layer pans or bundt pan if desired.

Bake 350° – 30 min.

Appendix 11 Floor Plans

Superintendent's House

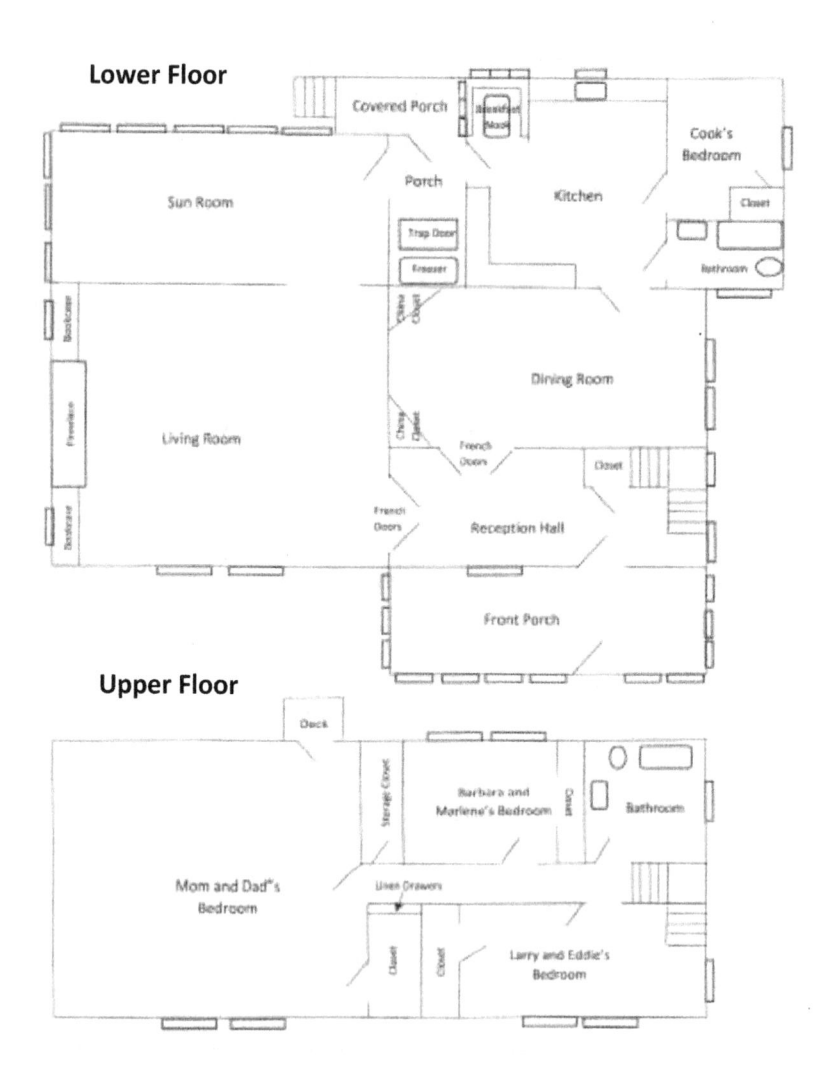

Lower Floor

Rooms labeled: Covered Porch, Breakfast Nook, Cook's Bedroom, Closet, Porch, Kitchen, Bathroom, Sun Room, Trap Door, Freezer, China Closet, Bookcase, Fireplace, Bookcase, Living Room, Dining Room, China Closet, French Doors, Closet, French Doors, Reception Hall, Front Porch

Upper Floor

Rooms labeled: Deck, Storage Closet, Barbara and Marlene's Bedroom, Closet, Bathroom, Mom and Dad's Bedroom, Linen Drawers, Closet, Closet, Larry and Eddie's Bedroom

248

Cinder Block House

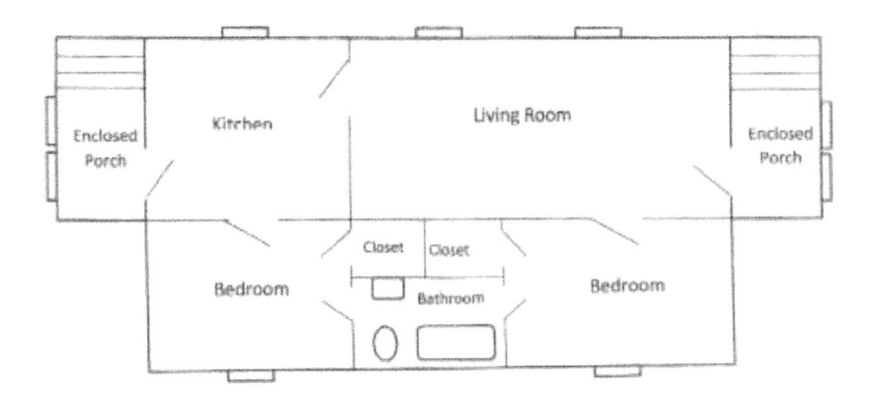

Appendix 12 - Photograph Credits

Cover
Dad and Mom Portrait, Picture courtesy of Marlene (Rutherford) Sutherland
Barbara Rutherford Graduation Portrait, Picture courtesy of Delores (Knez) Crow
Larry and Ed Graduation Portrait, Picture Courtesy of Barbara (Rutherford) Martin
Marlene Graduation Portrait, Picture courtesy of Marlene (Rutherford) Sutherland
Mount Harris Business District 1920, Courtesy of Herbert McCool, *Mt. Harris Echoes*, by Ruth Douglas Johnson, 1979, Pg. 19
Page iii
Dad and Mom Portrait, Picture courtesy of Marlene (Rutherford) Sutherland
Page iv
Family Picture, Picture Courtesy of Barbara (Rutherford) Martin
Page 1
Detail of a Miner with a Pipe, A miner with a pipe. P V & K Coal Company, Clover Mine, Lejunior, Harlan County, Kentucky. – NARA - [Public domain], via Wikimedia Commons
Page 3
Coke and Daisy Rutherford at the Superintendent's House, Picture Courtesy of Barbara (Rutherford) Martin
Page 4
Grandpa and Grandma Rutherford on their Wedding day, Picture Courtesy of Barbara (Rutherford) Martin
Page 5
Grandma Daisy Rutherford, Picture courtesy of Marlene (Rutherford) Sutherland
Page 6
Joseph L. Knez at the Ranch, Picture courtesy of Marlene (Rutherford) Sutherland
Page 7
Joseph L. Knez with his Coal Truck, Picture Courtesy of Barbara (Rutherford) Martin
Page 8
Marie (Mahowald) Knez 18 Years Old, Picture courtesy of Delores (Knez) Crow
Page 9
Coal Miners at the Knez Coal Mine, Picture courtesy of Delores (Knez) Crow
Page 12
Harris Mine at Mount Harris, Pagoda Quadrangle, Routt County, Colorado, 1912, United States Geographical Survey.
Mine Bridge and Tipple 1948, Courtesy of the Hayden Heritage Center
Mt. Harris with view of old wooden tipple in the foreground. Courtesy of Herbert McCool, , *Mt. Harris Echoes*, by Ruth Douglas Johnson, 1979, Pg. 15

Page 13
Detail of Wrinkled Miner, Scott's_Run,_West Virginia._(Unemployed_miner.)_-_NARA_- [Public domain], via Wikimedia Commons
Page 14
Mt. Harris Business District ca 1940's, Courtesy of the Hayden Heritage Center
Page 15
Mt. Harris Tokens and Scrip, Courtesy of the Hayden Heritage Center
Page 16
Joe Sena and Vic Zullian Main Trip, Harris Mine, Picture Courtesy of Julia Haske, *Mt. Harris Echoes,* by Ruth Douglas Johnson, 1979, Pg. 27
Page 17
Post Office Boxes, pixabay.com/en/post-office-old-vintage-building-649504/
Page 21
Mt. Harris tipple, Picture Courtesy of Elmer Wagner, *Mt. Harris Echoes,* by Ruth Douglas Johnson, 1979, Pg. 73
Page 23
Denver and Rio Grande Steam Locomotive, 1963, By Bill Bogle, Durango, CO. (eBay item photo front photo back) [Public domain], via Wikimedia Commons
Page 26
Yampa River, Picture Courtesy of Barbara (Rutherford) Martin
Page 27
Swinging Bridge, Courtesy of the Hayden Heritage Center
Page 28
Michael, Larry, Ian and James on an Expedition on the Yampa River, Courtesy of Larry Rutherford
Page 29
Rutherford Family Portrait, Ralph, Marie, Barbara and Marlene, Picture courtesy of Marlene (Rutherford) Sutherland
Page 30
Barbara and Marlene at the Cinder Block House, Picture courtesy of Marlene (Rutherford) Sutherland
Marie and Ralph, Picture courtesy of Marlene (Rutherford) Sutherland
Page 31
Roy Roger and Mary Hart - 1938, By Republic Pictures (eBay) [Public domain], via Wikimedia Commons
Sister Placide, Sister Columbiere, Marlene and Barbara, Picture courtesy of Marlene (Rutherford) Sutherland
Page 32
Mom, Ramona, Edith and Barbara, Picture Courtesy of Barbara (Rutherford) Martin
Page 33
Marlene – 1944, Picture courtesy of Marlene (Rutherford) Sutherland

Page 34
Barbara, Dad, Larry and Marlene at Cinder Block House, Picture Courtesy of Barbara (Rutherford) Martin
Barbara Sweeping the Walk, Picture Courtesy of Barbara (Rutherford)
Page 35
Barbara and Marlene at Druggist's House on Easter Sunday, Picture courtesy of Marlene (Rutherford) Sutherland
Page 36
Marlene and Larry at the Druggist's House, Picture courtesy of Marlene (Rutherford) Sutherland
Page 37
Larry and Ann Rutherford at Druggist's House, Picture courtesy of Marlene (Rutherford) Sutherland
Page 38
Superintendent's House, Picture courtesy of Marlene (Rutherford) Sutherland
Page 39
Hand Crank Wall Telephone, Pinterest.com, liveautioneers.com
Page 40
Superintendent's House in Winter, Picture Courtesy of Barbara (Rutherford) Martin
Page 41
Eddie and Larry at the Stone Fountain – Superintendent's House, Picture courtesy of Marlene (Rutherford) Sutherland
Larry in Halloween Costume, Picture courtesy of Marlene (Rutherford) Sutherland
Page 42
Eddie and Larry on a bicycle, Picture courtesy of Marlene (Rutherford) Sutherland
Page 43
Marlene, Eddie and Larry, Picture courtesy of Marlene (Rutherford) Sutherland
Eddie and Larry, Picture courtesy of Marlene (Rutherford) Sutherland
Page 44
Dad, Mom, Eddie and Larry, Picture courtesy of Marlene (Rutherford) Sutherland
Page 45
Mount Harris Grade School, Picture courtesy of Lawrence Rutherford
Page 46
Mrs. Harder and Mrs. Price, Picture Courtesy of Elmer Wagner, *Mt. Harris Echoes*, by Ruth Douglas Johnson, 1979, Pg. 46
Page 47
Mt. Harris class of 1950. Marlene Rutherford in the back row. Picture Courtesy of Ralph Rutherford, *Mt. Harris Echoes*, by Ruth Douglas Johnson, 1979, Pg. 45
Page 49
Mt. Harris cheerleaders, Marlene Rutherford, Beatrice Arroyo, Kathy Montoya, and Patsy Rolando, Picture Courtesy of Ralph Rutherford, *Mt. Harris Echoes*, by Ruth Douglas Johnson, 1979, Pg. 47

Page 50
Leonard Rutherford, Courtesy of the Hayden Heritage Center
Mom, Dad and Ed at Mesa Verde National Park 1955, Picture Courtesy of Barbara (Rutherford) Martin
Page 51
Loren Rutherford, Courtesy of the Hayden Heritage Center
Larry School Picture, Picture courtesy of Marlene (Rutherford) Sutherland
Page 52
Uncle Frances and Dad in Front of the Grade School, Picture courtesy of Marlene (Rutherford) Sutherland
Page 53
Witches Hat, http://savethephillipsfamily.com/2011/07/25/are-playgrounds-too-safe/
Page 55
Dad and Barbara at Graduation Ceremony, Picture Courtesy of Barbara (Rutherford) Martin
Marlene, school picture 56-57, Picture Courtesy of Barbara (Rutherford) Martin
Page 56
Hayden Union High School Band, Courtesy of The Hayden Heritage Center
Page 57
Loretto Heights College, By Jeffrey Beall [CC BY-SA 3.0 (https://creativecommons.org/licenses/by-sa/3.0)], from Wikimedia Commons
Page 58
Barbara at Grotto at Loretto Heights College, Picture Courtesy of Barbara (Rutherford) Martin
Page 60
Dad and Fr. Prinster at the Piano, Picture Courtesy of Barbara (Rutherford) Martin
Page 62
First Communion Class, Sr. Columbiere, Fr. Prinster, Larry, Picture courtesy of Marlene (Rutherford) Sutherland
Page 61
Father Prinster, Picture courtesy of Marlene (Rutherford) Sutherland
Page 63
Larry Dressed as Bishop at Druggist's House, Picture courtesy of Marlene (Rutherford) Sutherland
Altar in the Bedroom, Picture courtesy of Marlene (Rutherford) Sutherland
Page 65
Marlene and Barbara in Prom Dresses, Picture courtesy of Marlene (Rutherford) Sutherland
Page 66
Montgomery Ward Catalogue, Ebay.com
Larry in a Sailor Suit, Picture courtesy of Larry Rutherford

Page 67
Hair Styling Supplies, Picture Courtesy of Barbara (Rutherford) Martin
Page 68
Barbara in a Permanent, Picture Courtesy of Barbara (Rutherford) Martin
Barbara and Edie Fedinic with Roller Curls, Picture Courtesy of Barbara (Rutherford) Martin
Page 70
Girl Listening to the Radio, Franklin D. Roosevelt Library Public Domain Photographs
Page 71
Snowy Television Screen, envisioningtheamericandream.com
Page 72
Boys playing marbles, by doe-oakridge (Boys Playing Marbles Oak Ridge 1947) [Public domain], via Wikimedia Commons
Page 73
Cap gun, ebay.com
Page 74
Pet Owl, Picture courtesy of Marlene (Rutherford) Sutherland
Page 75
Johnny Sena, Isidro Arroyo, Larry Rutherford, Mike Arroyo, and Eddie Rutherford, Picture Courtesy of Ralph Rutherford, *Mt. Harris Echoes,* by Ruth Douglas Johnson, 1979, Pg. 143
Page 76
Abandoned Drive-in Theater, By Kevin [CC BY 2.0 creative commons.orglicenses by2.0, via Wikimedia Commons
Page 79
Jane Russell in Underwater, Ebay.com
Page 81
Spam can, By Qwertyxp2000 [CC BY-SA 4.0 (https://creativecommons.org/licenses/by-sa/4.0)], from Wikimedia Commons
Page 82
Barbara, Eddie, Marlene, Dad, Larry and Mom 1959, Picture Courtesy of Barbara (Rutherford) Martin
Page 86
Hayden Hospital, Picture courtesy of Marlene (Rutherford) Sutherland
Page 87
Yampa River Flood, Yampa River High Water Flood, Courtesy of Ellif Mosher, *Mt. Harris Echoes,* by Ruth Douglas Johnson, 1979, Pg. 108
Page 88
Dentist's Office, [Public domain], via Wikimedia Commons
Page 89
Polio Iron Lung Hospital Ward, Vintage es photo was taken at Rancho Los Amigos Hospital in Downey, California

Page 90
Tincture of Iodine, Ebay.com
Page 91
Larry "Smoking" a Pipe, Picture courtesy of Delores (Knez) Crow
Page 93
Vintage Lawn Mower, By UBC Library Digitization Centre [No restrictions], via Wikimedia Commons
Page 94
Larry, Marlene, Eddie and Barbara - Christmas in the early 1950's, Picture courtesy of Marlene (Rutherford) Sutherland
Page 97
Typical Sled, The Children's Museum of Indianapolis [CC BY-SA 3.0 (https://creativecommons.org/licenses/by-sa/3.0)], via Wikimedia Commons
Page 99
Golashes, Etsy.com
Page 101
Rattlesnake Jack Playing 3 Part Harmony on Three Trumpets, Picture Courtesy of Barbara (Rutherford) Martin
Rattlesnake Jack in the Boxing Ring, Courtesy of the Hayden Heritage Center
Page 102
Dad in Boxing Pose, Picture courtesy of Marlene (Rutherford) Sutherland
Page 103
Mom, Dad, Barbara, Marlene and Larry at the Druggist's House, Picture courtesy of Marlene (Rutherford) Sutherland
Mom, Barbara and Marlene, Picture courtesy of Marlene (Rutherford) Sutherland
Page 104
Uncle Francis on the Guitar and Dad on the Mandolin, Picture courtesy of Marlene (Rutherford) Sutherland
Page 107
Miner, Pennsylvania coal miners, by J. Collier [Public domain n], via Wikimedia Commons
Page 108
Fish Creek Falls, By Roy Brumback [CC BY-SA 3.0 (https://creativecommons.org/licenses/by-sa/3.0) or GFDL (http://www.gnu.org/copyleft/fdl.html)], from Wikimedia Commons
Page 109
Eddie, Larry and Ann Rutherford in the Mountains, Picture courtesy of Marlene (Rutherford) Sutherland
Page 110
Knez Homestead (abandoned), Pictures courtesy of Delores (Knez) Crow

Page 111
Coal Miner, Harry Fain, coal loader, right, talks to his section foreman upon completion of morning shift. Inland Steel Company – NARA - 541448 [Public domain], via Wikimedia Commons

Page 113
Delores Knez, Eddie and Larry, Picture courtesy of Marlene (Rutherford) Sutherland

Page 115
Coke and Daisy Rutherford in their Living Room, Picture courtesy of Marlene (Rutherford) Sutherland
Coke and Daisy Rutherford in their Kitchen, Picture courtesy of Marlene (Rutherford) Sutherland

Page 116
Aunt Dorris and Uncle Loren, Picture Courtesy of Barbara (Rutherford) Martin

Page 117
Juanita (Rutherford) and Alfred Camiletti, Picture courtesy of Marlene (Rutherford) Sutherland

Page 118
Uncle Antone, Uncle Raymond, Uncle Joseph and Grandpa at Juniper Hot Springs, Picture courtesy of Marlene (Rutherford) Sutherland

Page 119
Dad, Grandma Rutherford, Aunt Doris (Montieth) Rutherford, Francis Rutherford, Leonard Rutherford and Ralph Henderson. Picture courtesy of Marlene (Rutherford) Sutherland

Page 120
Uncle Bo and Aunt Marie Turner and Dad, Picture courtesy of Marlene (Rutherford) Sutherland

Page 121
Grandma Knez, Picture courtesy of Marlene (Rutherford) Sutherland

Page 122
Dad, Larry, Eddie and Aunt Margie, Picture courtesy of Marlene (Rutherford) Sutherland

Page 123
The Squires: Shirley, Daisy (Grandma), Edith, Annie, May, Margie, Andy, Coke (Grandpa), Rube, Frank, and Mike, Picture courtesy of Marlene (Rutherford) Sutherland

Page 124
Aunt Carol, Uncle Bo, Aunt Neat and Aunt Marie, Picture courtesy of Marlene (Rutherford) Sutherland

Page 125
Fred, Carol, Wanda and Ron McDonald, Picture Courtesy of Barbara (Rutherford) Martin

Page 126
Joseph, Raymond, Antone, Grandma, Grandpa, Mom and Louise, Picture courtesy of Marlene (Rutherford) Sutherland
Page 128
Roselin Carter, Picture courtesy of Marlene (Rutherford) Sutherland
Page 129
Mom and Aunt Grace, Picture courtesy of Marlene (Rutherford) Sutherland
Page 130
Mom and Aunt Grace, Picture courtesy of Delores (Knez) Crow
Page 131
Uncle Joseph, Aunt Virginia, Aunt Louise and Uncle Charley, Picture courtesy of Marlene (Rutherford) Sutherland
Page 132
Louise Fedinic, Helen Knez and Cleo Knez, Picture courtesy of Marlene (Rutherford) Sutherland
Page 133
Antone Knez, Dad, Larry and Raymond Knez, Picture courtesy of Marlene (Rutherford) Sutherland
Page 135
Grandma Knez, Uncle Joseph, Mom, Dad and Uncle Antone, Picture courtesy of Marlene (Rutherford) Sutherland
Page 138
Coal Miner with Black Face, [Public domain], via Wikimedia Commons
Page 139
Smiling Coal Miner, Pennsylvania_coal_miners, 1942 [Public domain], via Wikimedia Commons
Page 141
Craig, Colorado, Victory Way Facing West, www.panoramio.com
Page 143
Mom in front of Our House at 789 Tucker Street Craig, Picture courtesy of Marlene (Rutherford) Sutherland
Page 145
Larry and Eddie in back of Tucker St. House, Picture courtesy of Marlene (Rutherford) Sutherland
Page 147
Coal Miner, Mullens Smokeless Coal Company, [Public domain], via Wikimedia Commons
Page 149
Eddie – Third Grade, Picture courtesy of Marlene (Rutherford) Sutherland
Page 151
Coal Miner with Lunch Pail, [Public domain], via Wikimedia Commons

Page 153
Eddie Rutherford – Seventh Grade, Picture courtesy of Marlene (Rutherford) Sutherland

Page 156
Coal Miner Smoking a Pipe, Ben Shahn [Public domain], via Wikimedia Commons

Page 158
Edward – 1970, Picture Courtesy of Barbara (Rutherford) Martin

Page 161
MCHS Prom King and Queen c. 1965, Courtesy of the Museum of Northwest Colorado.

Page 162
Moffat County High School c. 1965, Courtesy of the Museum of Northwest Colorado

Page 165
Larry on a Bicycle, Picture courtesy of Marlene (Rutherford) Sutherland

Page 166
Dorothy and Joe Rotter, Mom and Dad, Eddie, Grandma Knez and Larry, Picture courtesy of Marlene (Rutherford) Sutherland

Page 170
Flower Garden and Grotto, Picture courtesy of Marlene (Rutherford) Sutherland

Page 173
Roger Hutton, Fr. Fraczkowski, Larry – Ad Altare Dei Award, Craig Empire Courier

Page 180
Statue of Liberty with Larry and Friends, Craig Empire Courier

Page 181
Larry, Dad, Ralph Henderson, Christy Camilletti and Eddie, Picture courtesy of Marlene (Rutherford) Sutherland

Page 189
African American Coal Miner, [Public domain], via Wikimedia Commons

Page 193
Ed with Lawn Mowers, Picture courtesy of Marlene (Rutherford) Sutherland

Page 194
Ed and Larry with Lawn Mowers on Buick, Picture courtesy of Marlene (Rutherford) Sutherland

Page 195
Dad Mowing the Grass, Picture courtesy of Marlene (Rutherford) Sutherland

Page 196
Family Picture - 1959, Picture Courtesy of Barbara (Rutherford) Martin

Page 198
Coal Miners on the Way to the Mine, [Public domain], via Wikimedia Commons

Page 200
Regis College, Denver, By Rpfitzgerald [CC BY-SA 3.0 (https://creativecommons.org/licenses/by-sa/3.0)], from Wikimedia Commons

Page 201
Edward and Larry, Picture courtesy of Marlene (Rutherford) Sutherland
Playing Cards in the Dorm Room, Picture courtesy of Marlene (Rutherford) Sutherland
Page 202
Larry Studying, Picture courtesy of Marlene (Rutherford) Sutherland
Page 204
Larry, Harvey Sprock, Gordon Valier and Snowman, Picture courtesy of Marlene (Rutherford) Sutherland
Page 206
Frances (Gastellum) Rutherford, Picture courtesy of Larry Rutherford
Page 208
Fran and Larry Going Out, Picture courtesy of Marlene (Rutherford) Sutherland
Page 215
2nd Lieutenant Rutherford, Picture courtesy of Marlene (Rutherford) Sutherland
Page 217
Ralph Rutherford, detail from Family Portrait, Picture courtesy of Marlene (Rutherford) Sutherland
Page 219
Marie Rutherford, Graduation Picture, Picture courtesy of Marlene (Rutherford) Sutherland
Page 233
Grandpa Knez with Deer, Picture courtesy of Marlene (Rutherford) Sutherland
Grandpa Knez Plowing, Picture courtesy of Marlene (Rutherford) Sutherland
Knez Coal Truck, Picture courtesy of Marlene (Rutherford) Sutherland
Page 234
Dad, Larry, Grandma Knez, Barbara and Marlene at Lake, Picture courtesy of Marlene (Rutherford) Sutherland
Marie Mahowald with a Friend, Picture courtesy of Marlene (Rutherford) Sutherland
Grandma Knez, Barbara and Marlene at the Ranch, Picture courtesy of Marlene (Rutherford) Sutherland
Page 235
Grandpa and Grandma Knez, Picture courtesy of Marlene (Rutherford) Sutherland
Knez Family, Picture courtesy of Marlene (Rutherford) Sutherland
Joseph, Marie, Antone, Louise and Raymond Knez, Picture courtesy of Marlene (Rutherford) Sutherland
Page 236
Roselin Carter Portrait, Picture courtesy of Marlene (Rutherford) Sutherland
Marie Carter, Picture courtesy of Marlene (Rutherford) Sutherland
Marie Carter Portrait, Picture courtesy of Marlene (Rutherford) Sutherland
Roselin Carter First Communion, Picture courtesy of Marlene (Rutherford) Sutherland

Page 237
Mom's Graduation 1939, Picture courtesy of Marlene (Rutherford) Sutherland
Mom and Dad at the Ranch, Picture courtesy of Delores (Knez) Crow
Dad on Rabbit Ears Pass, Picture courtesy of Marlene (Rutherford) Sutherland
Mom with a Hula Hoop, Picture courtesy of Delores (Knez) Crow
Page 238
Barbara and Marlene, Picture courtesy of Delores (Knez) Crow
Barbara and Marlene in front of a Car, Picture courtesy of Marlene (Rutherford) Sutherland
Eddie and Larry in front of the Depot, Picture courtesy of Marlene (Rutherford) Sutherland
Larry and Eddie along a Road, Picture courtesy of Marlene (Rutherford) Sutherland
Page 239
Uncle Antone in Army, Picture courtesy of Delores (Knez) Crow
Uncle Francis in Air Force, Picture courtesy of Marlene (Rutherford) Sutherland
Uncle Loren in Navy, Picture courtesy of Marlene (Rutherford) Sutherland
Uncle Leonard in Navy, Picture courtesy of Marlene (Rutherford) Sutherland
Page 240
Mom's Letter, Courtesy of Lawrence Rutherford
Page 243
Grandma Knez on the Ranch, Picture courtesy of Marlene (Rutherford) Sutherland
Page 245
Mom's Pie Crust Recipe, Courtesy of Barbara (Rutherford) Martin
Uncle Antone's Best Rum Cake Ever, Courtesy of Delores (Knez) Crow
Page 246
Dad's Pancake Recipe, Courtesy of Larry Rutherford
Mom's Caribbean Punch Bowl Recipe, Courtesy of Barbara (Rutherford) Martin
Page 247
Mom's Oatmeal cookie Recipe, Picture Courtesy of Barbara (Rutherford) Martin.
Mom's Poppy Seed Cake Recipe, Picture Courtesy of Barbara (Rutherford) Martin.

Psalm 77:3-6

I remembered God, and was distressed.
I contemplated, and my spirit groaned.

My eyes were kept from sleep:
I was troubled, and I could not speak.

I thought upon the days of old:
and I had in my mind the years gone by.

And I meditated in the night with my own heart:
and I contemplated and I swept my spirit.

Made in the USA
Middletown, DE
03 June 2023